The Feedback Pendulum

MICHAEL CHILES

First published 2021

by John Catt Educational Ltd,
15 Riduna Park, Station Road,
Melton, Woodbridge IP12 1QT

Tel: +44 (0) 1394 389850
Fax: +44 (0) 1394 386893
Email: enquiries@johncatt.com
Website: www.johncatt.com

Illustrations by Jason Ramasami

ISBN: 978 1 913622 19 0

Set and designed by John Catt Educational Limited

PRAISE FOR THE FEEDBACK PENDULUM

'Feedback is an essential topic for every teacher and school leader. It can impact positively or negatively on pupils' learning and on teachers' workloads. Too often though, schools are prone to damaging feedback fads. Perhaps the truth of these fads is that school teachers and leaders are uncertain about what feedback really means. Chiles' book is a helpful, pragmatic antidote to those all-too-common feedback fads. It synthesises a range of interesting evidence, voices from leaders and teachers, alongside practical approaches, to build a rich picture of what makes for effective feedback. As such, it provides vital food for thought for teachers and leaders of all stripes.'

Alex Quigley, teacher and blogger

'In *The Feedback Pendulum*, Michael Chiles provides insights and examples for tackling the fact that feedback, as we all know, does not always have the desired impact. This thought-provoking, practical book helps us get there. It is time, colleagues, to tackle head on the ghastliness and laziness of generic feedback. It is time to get shot of quality assurance that relies on book scrutiny and the amount of marking in pupils' books. It is time to have proper conversations about the power of feedback to improve the work of pupils and professionals: *The Feedback Pendulum* is a great starting point.'

Mary Myatt, education adviser, author and speaker

I loved reading this book. As Chris Moyse reminds us in his excellent foreword, the problem with feedback is that it doesn't always have the desired impact and all too often lands badly. This book is the perfect antidote. In recognising the importance of feedback, raising all the right questions and challenging our commonly held assumptions, it offers practical and evidence-informed solutions for how we can offer really effective feedback to pupils, teachers and parents. I love the spotlight case studies he has included from those working on the front line that really bring his ideas to life. Michael Chiles calls this book his feedback manifesto. If he were standing for election on this platform, he would certainly get my vote. I highly recommend this book – it has everything schools need to really make feedback a positive difference for pupils, which in the end is all that matters.'

Andy Buck, author and founder of Leadership Matters

Michael lifts the lid on feedback in a way that is simply superb and has never been attempted or achieved within any educational book before. With a forensic study of the way in which we use feedback at every layer of our profession, Michael reveals exactly how much of our most meaningful work relies upon the mechanism of feedback before offering an astute set of principles which will ensure teachers place feedback at the heart of all that they do. This book is set to be a key text for teachers to really get to grips with the relationship we have with feedback in schools, and I'm really excited to see what happens next.

Kat Howard, author and founder of @LitdriveUK

ACKNOWLEDGEMENTS

As always in anything that I do, I owe a big gratitude to my wife Sarah Thornton who has supported me throughout the writing of this and my previous book. It has become a running theme of me sitting for many hours with the laptop pondering over the research in the evening after a day at school.

I am extremely grateful to David Didau, Harry Fletcher-Wood and David Goodwin who, over the last few months, have provided guidance in the early drafts and challenged me to think about the different strands of feedback that underpin the book. This has helped me to improve and clarify my thinking to articulate how to approach feedback to pupils, teachers and parents. Also, a big thank you to Kat Howard, Jennifer Webb, Mary Myatt, Mark and Zoe Enser for taking the time to review it.

I also owe a big thank you to my colleagues and the Great Schools Trust who create a collaborative and supportive culture that has meant my own use of feedback as a teacher is effective and supports a work-life balance.

While the research and sharing of my own ideas I hope will be helpful for teachers as they consider feedback in their own roles, the opportunity to hear and see through the lens of other teacher's classrooms is for me invaluable. I am grateful to the fellow teachers, many of whom I have not had the privilege of meeting sharing their own experience of feedback in the spotlights that help to bring the book to life. Therefore, a big thank you to Sam Gibbs, Neil Almond, Emily Weston, Blake Harvard, Amy Searle, Jade Pearce and Jay Davenport.

I would like to thank Dr Joanne Riordan, the people involved in the Mulberry Bush Project and Action Jackson for their specialist spotlights and, of course, John Hattie for taking the time to share his thoughts on the feedback pendulum.

Finally, I am grateful to my editor Meena and my publishers John Catt for supporting me in producing and sharing this book with you. I hope that it provides a supporting guide to enable teachers to reflect on the role of feedback in education.

CONTENTS

FOREWORD BY CHRIS MOYSE

'I did then what I knew how to do. Now that I know better, I do better.' – Maya Angelou

Our lives are awash with feedback. In the broadest sense it includes any information you receive about yourself, how we learn about ourselves from our experiences and from other people. We have all been rated and graded, criticised and praised. As children we received frequent feedback from our teachers, our parents and maybe our siblings too. Not always positive feedback either. As adults we are constantly receiving feedback from friends, partners, family members and parents. Even strangers provide us with feedback; I receive feedback on my driving almost daily! However, if we are genuinely serious about getting better then we definitely need it. Feedback, therefore, is more than just useful – it's essential. It's hard to get motivated and difficult to stay motivated when you are unsure if you're on the right track. So giving clear, specific and frequent feedback is one of the most important responsibilities of any teacher, leader or manager.

It would seem that feedback is one of the few things in education that most people agree is important and worthwhile. The consensus from extensive research into its effect is that giving feedback has great benefits. The Education Endowment Foundation describe it as having 'high impact for very low cost, based on moderate evidence'. But giving feedback may not be as straightforward as we think. While there's certainly a great deal of research evidence on the effectiveness of feedback with some studies tending to show high effects on learning, there have been various studies which show a lower impact.[1]

---

1.   Kluger, A. N. and DeNisi, A. (1996) 'The effects of feedback interventions on performance: A historical review, a meta-analysis, and a preliminary feedback intervention theory', *Psychological Bulletin* 119 (2) pp. 254-284.

So feedback does seem to have a very wide range of effects. Therefore, it is important to understand the potential benefits and the possible limitations of feedback as a classroom approach. This essential and thoroughly researched book provides exactly that required insight into the evidence surrounding its use in our classrooms and how we might utilise feedback with much greater effect. It is definitely worth thinking harder about exactly what we mean by feedback and this extensive guide provides us all with a golden opportunity to do just that.

As teachers, we are also receivers of feedback as well as givers. Feedback awaits us on a lesson by lesson basis, usually from the students we teach but also from peers and managers. It does not matter if we like it or not, we are always on the receiving end of feedback, whether it be good or bad, constructive and useful or ill-informed and unhelpful. It is feedback to teachers that interests me the most as my daily role focuses on helping teachers become even better and, of course, feedback is crucial to that process.

The problem with feedback is that it doesn't always have the desired impact and all too often lands badly. As teachers, despite giving frequent feedback to our students, we generally don't like providing our peers with feedback especially if it requires a difficult or challenging discussion and, on the whole, we aren't always keen to receive it ourselves either. When we give feedback to our colleagues we often notice that they aren't very good at receiving it. But when we receive feedback from someone else, we often notice that they aren't very good at giving it!

Of course, we can train our teachers and leaders to give feedback far more effectively and far more often. That's relatively easy to do. But improving the skills of the giver won't achieve much if the receiver of the feedback is unable to absorb what is being said or is even unwilling to take the feedback. So becoming a better receiver is key. In a professional conversation it is the receiver who controls whether feedback is taken on, made sense of or brings about change. Therefore, we need to stop seeing feedback as something that is just given and focus much more on our ability to take it and use it. If the receiver is unwilling to receive the feedback, then it is highly unlikely that even the most skilful delivery will make a difference. So we will need to understand the barriers we have to it and have strategies to recognise, manage and overcome our resistance. Getting better at receiving feedback starts with understanding and managing the feelings we have when we get it.

Receiving feedback is hard. We want to grow, learn and flourish but we also have a longing to be accepted for who we are. As a result, even a relatively small suggestion can leave us feeling angry, dismissive, anxious or, at worst, threatened by the whole process. However, the good news is that receiving feedback well is a skill and with some careful thought, practise and application, we can get better at it. Being good at receiving feedback allows us to get better at our job. We, of course, need to understand how to give feedback better and one of the best ways to improve our ability to do so is to understand the agony of receiving it. Then we can embrace it and see it as an opportunity to further grow and develop.

This comprehensive and thoroughly researched guide to feedback will provide you with an opportunity to reflect on just how effectively you provide feedback to students and colleagues, providing you with a plethora of ideas and strategies to do so with even greater effect. But, remember, focus on the receiving just as much as the giving as learning is a shared responsibility but in the end it comes down to you.

Chris Moyse, Head of Staff Development at Bridgwater and Taunton College Trust and Managing Director of TLC Education Services Limited

INTRODUCTION

'I think it's very important to have a feedback loop, where you're constantly thinking about what you've done and how you could do it better.' – Elon Musk

During the early 20th century, the concept of feedback can be seen in writing when referring to electrical science: 'The secondary 20 of the transformer is connected by a feedback circuit 21 to the primary 16 of the transformer 15.'[2]

---

2. Merriam-Webster (no date) 'Word History: Get Looped In on 'Feedback'', *Merriam-Webster* [Online]. Retrieved from: www.bit.ly/38ycoSC

The most commonly recognised meaning of feedback – that relating to the social aspect of guiding people – was first used in the field of psychology during the 1940s. Shortly after World War II, the concept of feedback was being primarily used as a tool when discussing a person's performance with a task. It is this early definition that we now associate with when considering the social concept of feedback today. When I first started researching the role of feedback, I didn't fully appreciate the complexities the role feedback has in education and the degrees of variations in how effective it can be. The one thing that researchers do agree with is it can play a fundamental role in supporting learning at all levels.

In the series of chapters that follow, I will outline and delve into the research around the use of feedback as well as sharing what I believe, based on this research and my own experiences, are the key principles to effective feedback in education. The book explores the three core strands of feedback for pupils, teachers and parents. In Chapter 1, I explore the concept of feedback and how it has evolved in education, in particular how in the context of pupils it has become meshed with the process of marking.

The proceeding chapters then explore feedback across the three core strands of feedback to pupils, teachers and parents. In Chapter 2, the focus is on how we can support pupils to feedforward through the feedback we provide. This chapter unpacks the research around the role of feedback in supporting pupils to feedforward and how teachers can create a culture where the values of feedback are instilled in every pupil. In Chapter 3, the focus shifts to the role of feedback to teachers and why I believe there needs to be a shift in the CPD culture that exists in schools. In this chapter I explore the importance of feedback to support teacher education by giving teachers the time to develop through practising based on the feedback they receive.

In Chapter 4, the final strand for enhancing feedback in education through creating partnerships with parents to triangulate the feedback loop. The role parents play in supporting children to succeed demonstrates a positive correlation to pupil outcomes. In this chapter, I share several strategies that teachers and schools could explore to create positive partnerships with home. Finally, John Hattie, a world-renowned researcher who has produced extensive research evidence on feedback in education, as well as providing practical examples of how this can be applied in schools, shares his closing thoughts to this book. I am extremely grateful to him for taking the time to share his expertise in this field.

This is my manifesto for enhancing feedback in education.

1

LESS MARKING, MORE FEEDBACK: DOES THE PROCESS OF FEEDBACK NEED TO CHANGE?

'The simplest prescription for improving education must be dollops of feedback.' – John Hattie

Chapter checklist

✓ We receive and provide feedback verbally and written on a daily basis
✓ The way in which we process the feedback depends on how it is interpreted by the receiver

✓ The purpose of feedback is to develop, enlighten, coach and help people move forward

✓ Feedback should be phrased to help close the gap between what someone knows and what they should know

✓ Feedback has the potential to double the impact on learning

✓ In education, the role of feedback has been entangled in the pressure to provide numerical marks on classwork and collate evidence on teaching group performance

✓ Providing feedback is the first step, it needs to be acted upon to create the springboard for improvement

1.1 Setting the scene - feedback is everywhere...

It would probably be fair to assume that, as you have sat down to read this first chapter, you have been on the receiving end or the provider of feedback at some point during the day. If you were on the receiving end, take a minute to consider how you interpreted the feedback you were given. If you were the provider, did you get the expected response? Many variables would have affected how this feedback was received, how it was understood and, ultimately, whether it was acted upon.

Whether feedback is positive or negative, right or wrong, accepted or rejected, formal or informal, we are immersed in it daily. Every academic year pupils will receive feedback verbally and in written form based on evidence interpreted by teachers from hundreds of assignments, assessments, practice exams, questioning and classroom activities. Alongside pupil feedback, teachers are also receiving verbal and written feedback through peer observations, book scrutiny/ reviews, learning walks, as well as through engagement in CPD activities. Feedback is everywhere and plays a pivotal role in learning about ourselves as well as shaping how others perceive themselves.

The act of giving feedback is second nature to teachers and possibly something we take for granted. Whether that is directing our pupils on how to improve their work, correcting them on their behaviour, highlighting where their response may be wrong, or giving them praise for meeting the success criteria based on the learning intentions that have been set. It's difficult to imagine how teaching would be possible without giving feedback. Alongside the feedback teachers give to pupils, there is also the feedback interactions that take place with colleagues and contact made with parents to report on pupil progress through written reports or verbally through parental consultation evenings.

Feedback in schools is far and wide:

'Tom, remember you should be walking on the left-hand side of the corridor.'

'Sarah, when pupils enter the classroom have a retrieval activity ready for them to engage with.'

'Lucy has made significant improvements in her application to her studies in maths but there is room for improvement.'

'Ryan, explain what causes the end of the spit to curve over time.'

'How could you improve that letter to appeal to a wider audience?'

'When pupils entered the room, the opening task didn't have the desired effect on settling them. Why do you think that was?'

1.2 What do we mean by 'feedback' and what is its purpose?

It could be argued that it is impossible not to give feedback. It is a primary channel for us to communicate. Take a moment to think of a time when someone has done something that has caught your attention. You share your disapproval through a raised eyebrow, triggered when someone cuts across you in the street, or a quick thumbs up to acknowledge you are happy with someone, a smile, a nod of the head – all of these actions provides a form of feedback. Every time we speak or share a non-verbal cue with someone, the person is receiving feedback. Whether it is positive or negative, accepted or rejected, verbal or non-verbal, the act of giving feedback is all around us. It is a primary form in which we communicate and something that we do routinely, both consciously and unconsciously.

This was illustrated in a study conducted on pre-schoolers in 2002 where researchers explored the view that teaching is a natural cognition that, while complex, is something that we learn at an early age. The study tested the relations of children between the ages of 3-5 years. As children begin to talk they will often ask their parents to name an object. During these early stages of their childhood they are initiating a form of teaching and, in turn, receiving feedback from their parent as their understanding of the world around them is explored. In the study, children were observed teaching a board game to a peer. The game is summarised: 'The goal of the game is to collect a complete set of four cubes, each of different colour. The game involves taking turns and following a set of rules regarding the moves that are allowed in each turn.' (Strauss, Ziv and Stein, 2002)

Through explaining the rules and demonstration, the children were taught how to play the game. Following this, the children were asked whether they would be happy to teach a peer who was not familiar with the game. The study showed that right from an early age, children exhibit the ability to teach their peers and give feedback through demonstrations and verbal explanations.

In the context of schools, the primary purpose of feedback has evolved into an act which attempts to address the understanding gap based on how someone has performed relative to the anticipated goals. When it is provided to pupils, feedback is a channel of communication that uncovers what pupils have been successful in and whether they are on track to meet the learning intentions. It is the mechanism through which teachers can sharpen the lens for pupils to know where they have been successful in their work based on the learning intentions.

So, how can we define feedback in an education context? In exploring the extensive research conducted, here are a few definitions from the literature: 'Feedback is an objective description of a student's performance intended to guide future performance. Unlike evaluation, which judges performance, feedback is the process of helping our students assess their performance, identify areas where they are right on target, and provide them with tips on what they can do in the future to improve in areas that need correcting.' (Miser, no date)

In another research paper, feedback is defined as: 'A process whereby learners obtain information about their work in order to appreciate the similarities and differences between the appropriate standards for any given work, and the qualities of the work itself, in order to generate improved work.' (Boud and Molloy, 2013)

'Information provided by an agent (e.g. teacher, peer, book, parent, self, experience) regarding aspects of one's performance or understanding.' (Hattie and Timperley, 2007)

'Feedback is to communicate an individual status in relation to a standard behavior or professional practice.' (Veloski et al, 2006)

'Feedback is information with which a learner can confirm, add to, overwrite, tune or restructure information in memory, whether that information is domain knowledge, meta-cognitive knowledge, beliefs about self and tasks, or cognitive tactics and strategies.' (Butler and Winne, 1995)

'Effective feedback may be defined as feedback in which information about previous performance is used to promote positive and desirable development.' (Archer, 2010)

In 2003, Mutch defined the purpose of feedback as a key mechanism in 'the development and enhancement of learning', and Orrell (2006) suggests that the role of feedback in education is the 'cornerstone of all learning'. Shute (2007) wrote that 'formative feedback represents information communicated to the learner that is intended to modify the learner's thinking or behavior for the purpose of improving learning'.

While these definitions have their differences there is a common thread that runs through which is the focus on improvement in reaching the desired goals set to enable learning based on prior performance. Feedback is an essential part of learning. To gain a broader understanding of how teachers interpret the concept of feedback in education, I asked what the word feedback meant to teachers. As expected, there were differences in opinion but there were several words that were mentioned more frequently than others as illustrated on the next page.

Guidance
Understanding
Improvement
Correcting
Judgement
Change
IdentifyingGaps
Performance DesirableChanges
Goals
Coaching
Development
Information
Help Differences
Support

Feedback focuses on providing information on current performance based on how well the person has met the intentions of the original task. This is only one aspect of the learning process. Throughout our day-to-day lives we receive feedback on our performance, but for improvement we need to know how to do better. We need constructive advice on how we can move forward to achieving the aim. This is where providing constructive comments that enable people to feedforward is crucial to creating the right conditions for effective and efficient feedback that facilitates learning. For example, I can tell a pupil they didn't explain the full sequence for the formation of a wave-cut platform through the use of physical processes that act on the landscape but unless I provide the constructive advice on how to do better, they will repeat the same mistake when they come to try and explain the formation of another landform.

Hattie and Timperley's research paper 'The Power of Feedback' set out the parameters for an effective model of feedback, illustrated by the adjacent diagram.

Hattie and Timperley's Model of Feedback

Purpose
To reduce discrepancies between current understandings/performance and a desired goal

THE DISCREPANCY CAN BE REDUCED BY

Teachers	Students
Providing appropriate challenging and specific goals	Increased effort and employment of more effective strategies
OR	OR
Assisting students to reach them through effective strategies	Abandoning, blurring or lowering the goals

EFFECTIVE FEEDBACK ANSWERS THREE QUESTIONS

Feed 'up'	Feed 'back'	Feed 'forward'
Where am I going? (The Goals)	How am I going?	Where am I going? (The goals)

EACH FEEDBACK QUESTION WORKS AT FOUR LEVELS

Task level	Process level	Self-regulation level	Self level
How well tasks are understood/ performed	The main process needed to understand/perform tasks	Self-monitoring, directing, and regulating of actions	Personal evaluations and affect (usually positive) about the learner

1.3 The research on feedback over time

There has been extensive academic research on the power of feedback from Lysakowski and Walberg in 1982 and Hattie in 2009. In reading several of these research papers on feedback, there is one thing they have in common, which is the potential positive relationship that feedback can have on performance. In Hattie's meta-analysis of over 1200 studies, the role of feedback in supporting improvement leads to academic achievement. Hattie's findings indicated that feedback has the potential to double the impact on learning, with an average effect size of 0.81. The evidence taken from a range of studies reinforces how the use of feedback can be a fundamental cog in driving one of the wheels of our education but equally one of the most variable in its effectiveness for teachers, pupils and parents.

The following graph illustrates some of these research studies that illustrate the effect size that general feedback has on performance. Whilst there are variations in the effect size across the seven research studies, they were all positive.

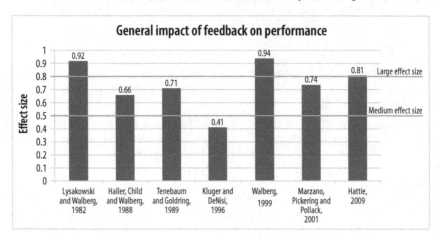

When mapped against other study strategies, feedback has the power to positively contribute towards boosting learning.

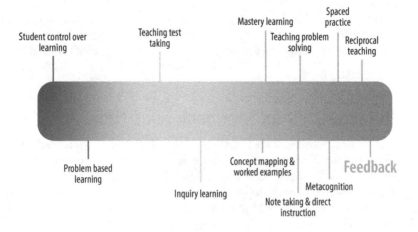

1.4 The challenges of feedback – the unstable ship

It could be argued that the variability in the effectiveness of feedback can be attributed to the degree to which the word has been interpreted, as indicated by the question I asked. There is an entrenched belief that marking, planning and the use of data are effective proxies for making judgements on teacher performance. These proxies have been allocated high stakes within schools to measure and quantify if a teacher is performing effectively. If a teacher is following a marking policy, then they must be an effective teacher. Of course, to say that a teacher's effectiveness is pre-determined by their ability to follow a marking policy is nonsense. Meeting the requirements of the marking policy does not necessarily equate to contributing towards having an effective influence on pupil learning. The desire to control and measure teaching through these proxies leads to resentment and teachers playing lip service to the process. Over time, this has created lethal mutations of a great emphasis on written marking. This was emphasised by David Didau (2016) in one of his blogs reflecting on the government workload review report. The main issue for David was the use of the word 'marking' and not 'feedback': 'I am particularly concerned by the report's opening sentence: "Effective marking is an essential part of the education process." I lobbied hard for this to be changed to "effective feedback is an essential part of the education process and marking is just one possible way for teachers to provide feedback to students".'

In David's blog the key message was the potentially harmful connotations associated with the emphasis on the use of the word marking as an 'essential' part of education. Rightly so, David points out that less marking can lead to greater and potentially more effective feedback, highlighting that many successful countries do not apply an emphasis on the use of marking to support learning. Reflecting on my own practice, I remember not writing a single comment on one of my pupils books in Year 11 for the whole academic year. I used other channels to provide the appropriate feedback she needed. Needless to say, she achieved an A*.

From this discussion, the continued reliance on the use of marking as a proxy for teacher performance leads to questionable impacts on learning. The more teachers come to resent the process of marking, the greater the variability in its effectiveness, reducing it further when it already has a low overall effect size. A move from marking policies to feedback policies, where marking is not the main driver for providing feedback would be a more effective approach to supporting pupils learning and teacher wellbeing.

The research demonstrates that there is a difference between giving feedback and it being acted on. Teachers provide pupils with feedback all the time, but it is the acting on the feedback that contributes to pupils' learning. Sharing feedback with pupils but with no follow-up is like baking a cake and leaving the baking powder out of it but expecting it to still rise nicely. The power of feedback is determined by the power of the follow-up. As teachers, we give pupils feedback, in written form and verbally throughout the day, but to what extent do pupils effectively act on the feedback? This was emphasised by Shute's report on the role of formative feedback, 'good feedback can significantly improve learning processes and outcomes, if delivered correctly'. The key phrase here in Shute's research report is 'if delivered correctly' because on the flip-side if delivered ineffectively it can significantly degrade learning. As we have already discussed, the excessive dependence on the use of marking to give feedback can have negative effects on learning.

Building on the research of Ames (1992) and Hattie and Timperely (2007), they concluded that:

- what feedback describes is the key to its impact.
- feedback that directs attention to the intended learning has a positive impact on achievement.
- feedback is most effective when it points out strengths in the work and gives guidance for improvement. (Chappuis, 2012)

In many schools up and down the country, feedback and marking have been used interchangeably with the latter taking the stage in an emerging high-stakes accountability process to demonstrate pupil progress. In a report by the University of Waikato on the use of feedback to promote student learning, it was highlighted that pupils and teachers had concerns about the feedback process. These concerns, along with those of parents which I have added, are illustrated on the following pages.

Pupil concerns	Teacher concerns	Parental concerns
• The feedback is not clear, and they do not understand. • The feedback does not show them how to improve their work. • The purpose of the feedback is unclear. • There is too much feedback. • There is too little feedback. • The feedback is too late to be helpful. • The criteria are unclear. • The feedback comments are demotivating. • There is little opportunity to discuss the feedback.	• Pupils do not read the feedback comments because they are more interested in the grade. • Pupils are not interested in receiving feedback. • Providing feedback to pupils is too time-consuming. • Difficult to decide how much feedback is useful for pupils. • Unsure of the best format to provide feedback to pupils. • Pupils do not know what to focus on from teacher feedback comments. • We do not know how to get pupils to understand the criteria.	• There are too many subjects to grasp what my child needs to do. • The comments to my child are unclear. • I want to know whether my child is on or off-target. • I want to know what my child needs to do to improve and achieve their target grade.

This issue was echoed by the government's 2016 Independent Teacher Workload Group who indicated the problems with the workload around marking. In the report, some of the key issues with marking were identified as follows:

- Providing written feedback on pupils' work has become disproportionately valued by schools and has become unnecessarily burdensome for teachers.
- The quantity of feedback should not be confused with the quality. The quality of the feedback, however given, will be seen in how a pupil can tackle subsequent work.
- Marking is a vital element of teaching, but when it is ineffective it can be demoralising and a waste of time for teachers and pupils alike. In particular, we are concerned that is has become common practice for teachers to provide extensive written comments on every piece of work when very little evidence exists that this improves pupil outcomes in the long term.
- A cultural challenge of spending hours marking makes you a good teacher and the more pages of feedback you write, the more effective the feedback.
- There is no 'one-size-fits-all' approach. A balance needs to be struck between a core and consistent approach and trusting teachers to focus on what is best for their pupils and circumstances.
- Schools should aim to shrink the importance that marking has gained over other forms of feedback and stop unnecessary and burdensome practice.
- Ineffective marking can be dispiriting, for both teacher and pupil, by failing to encourage and engender motivation resilience.
- Marking has become disjointed from the learning process, failing to help pupils improve their understanding. This can be because work is set and marked to a false timetable and based on a policy of following a mechanistic timetable, rather than responding to pupils' needs.
- Providing written feedback on a pupil's work has become disproportionately valued by schools and has become unnecessarily burdensome for teachers.

The issues associated with marking and teacher workload were further emphasised in the 2019 teacher workload survey. The average number of hours spent on marking/correcting pupils' work increased from 6 to 8.2 hours for primary teachers and 6.3 to 8 hours for secondary teachers. For me this indicates the role of marking and feedback has become intertwined with many school policies set up to please the wrong audience – Ofsted – or to demonstrate evidence of pupil progress to senior leaders.

This leads to high stakes associated with marking to check that teachers have provided pupils with a specific form of feedback as directed by the policy in the set timeframes. The myths around the quantity and frequency of marking schools were expected to demonstrate were clarified by Ofsted (2018) in their myth-busting document in October 2014: 'Ofsted recognises that marking and feedback to pupils, both written and oral, are important aspects of assessment.

However, Ofsted does not expect to see any specific frequency, type or volume of marking and feedback; these are for the school to decide through its assessment policy. Marking and feedback should be consistent with that policy, which may cater for different subjects and different age groups of pupils in different ways, in order to be effective and efficient in promoting learning.'

The historical problem is that many of these school policies lack the focus on addressing the needs of the right audience, the pupils. This supports Hattie and Timperley's claim that while feedback has the power to improve learning, some types of feedback are more powerful than others, with marking potentially one of the least effective and efficient at promoting learning.

In *The CRAFT of Assessment*, I outlined a whole school approach to assessment for learning. The 'F' and 'T' of CRAFT involved the combination of supporting pupils to feedforward using target-driven improvements. When reflecting on the issues around the use of marking, I shared my marking mayhems of the past.

- **Ecocentric-driven marking** – it was encouraged that teachers should provide a 'well done' or 'excellent effort' when providing feedback on pupil's work. There was one point where teachers had to find a positive spin on the work regardless.
- **Deep (triple) marking** – providing pupils with feedback on a task, then giving them time to respond to the feedback in a different colour pen, I remember in one school I worked in we had three different coloured pens for this process – red for initial marking, purple for pupils to respond and green for re-marking. I would then re-mark the response pupils made from my initial feedback.
- **Quantity was king over quality** – the more written comments throughout exercise books the more effective I was perceived as a teacher. I would spend hours marking books writing the same comments for the same mistakes repeatedly. On reflection, I wasted many hours in the early parts of my career writing similar comments on pupil's work.
- **A 'mark' and 'grade' focus** – in some schools I worked in there was a requirement to provide pupils with a mark, level or grade every two weeks for a targeted piece of work. This would often be an extended piece of writing. There are many issues with this because the use of marks or grades can be a distractor taking away the focus which is to know how to improve.
- **Extensive next steps in assessments** – the infamous two stars and a wish or WWW/EBI was part of several feedback policies. While providing positive comments on the work and suggested improvements is not all bad, it is the nature in which many of these policies have been set up. It becomes a distraction to find something positive and comments on how the work can be improved.

Feedback and the memory model

In *How We Learn*, Stanislas Dehaene suggests there are four pillars of learning with each pillar playing a key role in the ability for us to be able to stabilise our mental constructions. He indicates that if teachers can mobilise each of the four pillars in their pupils it will create the right conditions for learning. I provide a summary and the wider context associated with his four pillars of attention, active engagement, error feedback and consolidation which follow.

ATTENTION

It seems an obvious point that to create the right environment for pupils to learn they need to pay attention to their teacher. However, the extent to which this pillar may become a focus for teachers could be of considerable variability. In this new digital era, mobile phones are a significant distraction to our daily lives. There have been occasions when people are so oblivious to their surroundings that they have almost walked into me or they have zoned out of a conversation because they are replying to a text message or surfing social media. At this point, they struggle to recall the conversation that had taken place just a few seconds or minutes beforehand. Multitasking is a myth that continues to prevail with scientists indicating that when we do attempt to multitask one of the operations will be hindered. There is the potential to assume that pupils are paying attention in our lessons but there are times when they can become easily distracted by the subtle events going on around them, a bird flying past the window, the whispering of another pupil seating near them, or the movement of people in the corridor. Each one of these interactions can easily distract our attention and subsequently lead to distorting the ability for us to learn, ultimately leading to knowledge gaps.

ACTIVE ENGAGEMENT

I am sure you can think of a time when you have taught a class that is 'compliant' to your rules or you've walked into a classroom where it is completely silent. Pupils can be compliant to rules and at the same time be passive. When pupils are passive in lessons the rate of learning diminishes. If pupils are to learn effectively and engage with the feedback received by teachers, they need to be actively involved in the lesson. How many times have you asked a question to a pupil and they had zoned out for a few minutes during your explanation? The lack of active engagement works hand in hand with attention. As Stanislas indicates in his book, this is not about pupils' physical movements but the active engagement of their brains in receiving and encoding the new concepts and processes explained to them by their teacher. All 30 pupils may be very still physically but their thoughts varying considerably from some being actively involved in the lesson to others disengaged and passive. While we should aim for pupils to be actively engaged in the lesson to be able to receive and process our feedback, this active engagement should not be confused with discovery-based learning. The latter being a form of pedagogy that studies have demonstrated when we leave pupils to discover for themselves the rate of learning is reduced.

ERROR FEEDBACK

The role of error feedback is key to learning. If a person is to learn they need to receive feedback quickly and accurately. While receiving this feedback quickly and accurately is important, creating the conditions where there is a collective belief that no one learns without making mistakes is equally important. Stanislas highlights that error feedback should not be confused with punishment because this can be counterproductive in promoting learning. In this case, teachers should look to create school and classroom environments where making an error is part of learning. When we learn to ride a bike and the stabilisers are removed, we will inevitably fall off. When we fall off, we need informative feedback on how to improve to move forward, we should not be punished. We learn that to improve we must keep getting back on and practising. Therefore, we should not confuse error feedback with punishment. The use of grades could be a form of punishment.

CONSOLIDATION

The act of consolidation, the fourth pillar is an important component for efficient and effective learning. The more pupils spend time reflecting on what have learnt the more it becomes automatic. I will often ask pupils the question related to the location of apps on their mobile phone. I bet all of you know where a specific app is located on your smartphone without too much thought. On most occasions, almost all pupils nod and put their hand up. The more we practice consolidating knowledge taught the more automated it becomes. This is something emphasised by Stanislas in his book: 'Repeated practice turns control over to the motor cortex and especially the basal ganglia, a set of subcortical circuits that record our automatic and routine behaviour.'

As we begin to learn something new it requires conscious effort. The more we receive feedback, modify our approach and practice the more automated it becomes and the effort it takes begins to diminish. The role of feedback in this process of moving from conscious to unconscious recall is important in helping to free up working memory.

Establishing a culture for the principles of feedback

Creating the right conditions where pupils, teachers and parents want to receive, seek out, use and give feedback is important to ensure that it is effective and efficient at supporting learning. On the whole, people want to strive to improve and feedback can be a powerful tool in supporting this process. For this to be meaningful, teachers and pupils should be actively engaged in the feedback process. Some of the key feedback principles that I believe can support an effective and efficient culture of feedback in schools are unpicked as this book develops and presents several strategies that teachers can use to implement them.

TIMELY

There is a tendency for school feedback policies to expect teachers to provide some form of detailed feedback on a mini-assessment every two weeks. The problem with this, like many of these over-burdensome policies, this can lead to shoehorning a focus on providing extensive written feedback on these assessments to meet the demands of the policies. Secondly, we know that learning is not uniform or predictable, it's messy. If we leave providing feedback to these set timescales it can negatively impact learning. On the other hand, a degree of delay could benefit the long-term retention of knowledge. This leads to the debate between the use of immediate and delayed feedback. So, is there an optimum time in which teachers should provide pupils with feedback?

When it comes to reviewing the research on the timing of feedback there are conflicting results on whether feedback should be provided immediately or delayed with no definitive suggestion of how these to variables of time affect learning. The use of either immediate or delayed feedback provide their own positives and negatives. Soderstrom and Bjork (2014) suggest that there is evidence to support that 'delaying, reducing and summarising feedback can be better for long-term learning than providing immediate, trial-by-trial feedback'.

Immediate feedback is usually something that is provided after pupils have completed a task while delayed feedback may be provided many minutes, hours, weeks or months after the completion of a task. As Soderstorm and Bjork indicated, delaying feedback can be beneficial for long-term retention of learning by reducing proactive interference, which in turn allows the initial error to be forgotten and then re-encoded with no interference (Shute, 2007). Many of the researchers who support delayed feedback build on what was introduced by Kulhavy and Anderson (1972). They proposed the concept of the interference-perseveration hypothesis. This suggests that whatever the initial errors that were made, these do not affect the correct information if provided following a delayed period. The original errors that may have formed are likely to be forgotten and will not interfere with retention. In contrast to delayed feedback, researchers in support of immediate feedback suggest that the earlier pupils are provided with constructive comments, the more efficient the knowledge retention will be.

The positive impact of immediate feedback has been seen, particularly in maths. This led to the suggestion by Schroth (1992) and Corbett and Anderson (2001) that the role of immediate vs delayed feedback is dependent upon the task. They suggested that delayed feedback is more effective for encouraging the transfer of learning, while immediate feedback for developing procedural skills, such as those in maths. This suggested link between timing and the effectiveness of feedback was further reviewed by Mathan and Koedinger (2002), concluding that 'the effectiveness of feedback depends not on the main effect of timing, but the nature of the task and the capability of the learner'. This led to further exploration and the observation that as the difficulty of the task decreases, the longer the delay in the feedback.

Immediate feedback	Delayed feedback
It is effective to provide instant mistake correction during task performance; this may lead to quicker accomplishment.	It is effective to provide delayed mistake correction during the processing of a task when it requires a longer duration to accomplish the task.
Its effects are likely to be more powerful at the task level.	Its effects are likely to be more powerful at the process level.
It is useful for attaining easy learning outcomes because it involves a shorter degree of processing about the task.	It is useful for attaining difficult learning outcomes because it involves a greater degree of processing about the task.

For feedback to be effective, it should be through a variety of different forms that are part of an ongoing process. It should be something that is not allocated a timescale. For this to happen, teachers should have the autonomy to provide feedback as and when it is needed. For this to happen teachers should be equipped with the strategies that will enable them to recognise when pupils need feedback. In the next chapters of this book, I will unpick strategies that can be used to build in opportunities for regular feedback.

RECEPTIVE CULTURE

For feedback to be efficient and effective for both pupils and teachers, there needs to be a culture established where the receiver wants to embrace the feedback. People can be easily defensive when on the receiving end of feedback and this can be difficult in supporting someone to develop. No matter how skilful the person is at delivering the feedback, if the person is not willing to listen and absorb the feedback it will not support learning and in turn improvement. Typically, pupils would rather be seen as lazy than stupid because if they don't try this provides them with what they perceive as a credible excuse for failing. 'Tom, the main opening at the top of a volcano is the crater.' 'Oh, yes. I knew that I just forgot to label it.'

Didau (2014) highlights that this is because people often see effort as something flexible whereas intelligence is perceived as fixed. We are either clever or not. Of course, we know that this is essentially untrue. We can exemplify this concept with that of an athlete. We know that athletes can improve through regular practice and over time improve their personal best or set new world records. So, why do so many people not align practice with getting cleverer? A possible reason for this is the attribution theory. The table (Wiliam, 2011, p. 110) provides an overview of the results of a survey when exploring the role of effort being attributed to levels of success.

Attribution of	Ego	Task
Expenditure of effort	• To do better than others • To avoid doing worse than others	• Interest • To improve performance
Success	• Ability • Performance of others	• Interest • Effort • Experience of previous learning

The evidence suggests that if we are to create a receptive feedback culture where pupils are willing to embrace the feedback given it should be based on the task and not that of the pupils themselves. From Dweck's research, she suggested our perception of success or failure is dependent upon the following three factors:

- Personalisation: the extent to which we believe success is influenced by internal or external factors.
- Stability: whether success if perceived to be transient or long-lasting.
- Specificity: whether success is interpreted as being likely to lead to success in other areas.

Attribution	Success	Failure
Personalisation	**Internal:** 'It was a good piece of work.' **External:** 'The teacher likes me.'	**Internal:** 'It wasn't a very good piece of work.' **External:** 'The teacher doesn't like me.'
Stabilty	**Stable:** 'I'm good at the subject.' **Unstable:** 'I was lucky with the questions that came up.'	**Stable:** 'I'm rubbish at the subject.' **Unstable:** 'I didn't bother revising.'
Specificity	**Specific:** 'I'm good at that but that's the only thing I'm good at.' **Global:** 'I did well at that so I'll do well at everything.'	**Specific:** 'I'm no good at that, but I'm good at everything else.' **Global:** 'I'm rubbish at everything.'

(Wiliam, 2011, p. 117)

Didau suggests that if we are going to provide pupils with feedback that prompts greater effort, we should be considering the following:

1. Target feedback to increase task commitment.
2. Design feedback that will be attributed to internal factors that pupils can control.
3. Design feedback that makes pupils consider unstable factors that are dependent on effort.
4. Make feedback as specific as possible (Didau, 2014) (this links back to one of the other key principles that I have already discussed earlier of making feedback granular).

Creating a receptive feedback culture takes time but so often the focus is on upskilling those who are giving the feedback. Instead, we should look to develop pupils and teachers in receiving feedback. This is emphasised by Douglas Stone and Sheelia Heen: 'Creating the pull is about mastering the skills required to drive our own learning, it's about how to recognise and manage our own resistance, how to engage in feedback conversations with confidence and curiosity, and even when the feedback seems wrong, how to find insight that might help us grow.' As Wiliam pointed out, we want pupils to believe that greater effort is up to them and through receiving and accepting feedback they can do something about it to improve.

GRANULAR - 'LESS IS MORE'

In the past, it has been a necessity to provide several targets both verbally and written to pupils on their work, as well as providing several targets for teachers following an observation. This can lead to the next steps becoming overwhelming and can be a contributing factor for the reason pupils and teachers reject feedback. Where possible we want to create the conditions that encourage people to not push back on the feedback they receive. If there is too much feedback or it lacks clarity, the next steps can seem unachievable and lead to people pushing back. The feedback provided should be granular, razor-sharp and specific so that the receiver, the pupil or the teacher knows exactly how to improve. It should be clearly linked to the original intentions. They need to feel that the next steps are within their grasp. After all, as humans we want to feel we can achieve something, we want to feel it is in our grasp and then when we have made the steps towards improvement, it makes us feel good. In turn, it makes us want to receive, process and move forward with feedback in the future.

Effective	Ineffective
A specific, granular target that is focused on the next step. *'Remember an excellent essay will include references to the writer. For example, ...'*	Next steps are vague and unhelpful. *'Add more detail to your explanation.'* *'Write more to this point that you have made.'*
The feedback will focus on the elements of the work that demonstrates understanding with constructive comments to direct improvement.	The feedback focuses mainly on where the pupil made incorrect responses.
Creates an opportunity for self/peer assessment to encourage pupils to take responsibility.	The feedback provided is too reliant on extrinsic rewards such as stickers.

SUPPORTS SELF-REGULATION

For feedback to be effective pupils should be actively involved in the process and be able to assess themselves through a clear understanding of how to improve. We should look to create opportunities that build an understanding of their own work through guided feedback. After all, it is only the pupil who can make the necessary changes to their classwork to bring about improvement in learning and, in turn, their performance. The combined research on self-regulated learning and cognitive load theory provides several working definitions, including: 'Thoughts, feelings and actions that are planned and adapted to the attainment of personal goals' (Zimmermann, 2000).

'Self-regulated learning is an active and constructive process in which a learner plans, monitors, and exerts control over his or her own learning process' – Kostons, Van Gog and Paas (2012).

Zimmermann (2010) provided further guidance on what we would expect to see from a pupil who demonstrated evidence of being a self-regulated learner: 'These learners are proactive in their efforts to learn because they are aware of their strengths and limitations and because they are guided by personally set goals and task-related strategies, such as using an arithmetic addition strategy to check the accuracy of solutions to subtraction problems. These learners monitor their behavior in terms of their goals and self-reflect on their increasing effectiveness. This enhances their self-satisfaction and motivation to continue to improve their methods of learning.'

The act of self-regulation can be expressed in the following ways:

- Setting goals for learning
- Concentrating on instruction
- Using effective strategies to organise ideas
- Using resources effectively
- Monitoring performance
- Managing time effectively
- Holding positive beliefs about one's capabilities (Schunk and Ertmer, 2000)

The concept of self-regulation can be split into the following core elements.

Affective capacities – moods, feelings and emotions	Cognitive capacities – beliefs, perceptions and knowledge	Metacognitive skills – memory, attention and problem solving

One way teachers can support self-regulation is sharing the learning intentions and the associated success criteria at the beginning of a learning sequence. This will enable pupils to check their work and make necessary improvements before sharing with their peer or teacher to build resilience.

The Education Endowment Fund released a guidance report on Metacognition and Self-Regulated Learning synthesising a range of research-based evidence to provide teachers with seven key recommendations to promote this with learners.

- **Recommendation 1** – Teachers should acquire the professional understanding and skills to develop their pupils' metacognitive knowledge.
- **Recommendation 2** – Explicitly teach pupils metacognitive strategies, including how to plan, monitor and evaluate their learning.
- **Recommendation 3** – Model your thinking to help pupils develop their metacognitive and cognitive skills.
- **Recommendation 4** – Set an appropriate level of challenge to develop pupils' self-regulation and metacognition.
- **Recommendation 5** – Promote and develop metacognitive talk in the classroom.
- **Recommendation 6** – Explicitly teach pupils how to organise and effectively manage their learning independently.
- **Recommendation 7** – Schools should support teachers to develop their knowledge of these approaches and expect them to be applied appropriately.

In the next chapter we will explore several strategies teachers can use to support metacognition and self-regulated learning.

Specialist Spotlight: Feedback and the future

ACTION JACKSON, MOTIVATIONAL SPEAKER

Action Jackson is an award-winning motivational speaker, author, television talk show host and a mentor. He has spent the last 20 years travelling across the UK and the world, motivating and empowering people. His mission is to create a world where young people wake up happy and go to bed fulfilled. His passion is to see young people flourish in their talents as leaders, impacting our society for good.

You can find him tweeting as @ActionJackson

In a world where young people are feeling increasingly insecure about their identity and place in society, how we educate and empower them is crucial. We are living at a time of accelerated change, overwhelming complexity and tremendous competition. The speed of change now means we must do more learning to catch-up with the avalanche of information coming at us daily. This exchange of information is a sign that things are changing in industries around the world, which gives rise to competition. If our young people are not adequately equipped, they will be faced with overwhelming complexities. With this mammoth task ahead of them, how they feel about their performance in class is crucial and this feeling comes from feedback.

Feedback = feelings

Your feedback as an educator should help your students raise the BAR to achieve the best of what they can achieve in your subject. The word 'BAR' is a learning aid that helps drive the principle deeper into your mind.

THE 'B' IS FOR 'BELIEF'

This is the sense of certainty a young person has about their capability and your subject. If their beliefs are negative it will have a massive affect on their performance. Our beliefs propel our actions in all we do. If a student believes that she is not capable of something, no matter what's placed in front of her, she won't progress because her belief system is the power behind her potential to perform well.

Henry Ford is quoted to have said: 'If you think you can or you think you cannot, you're right.' This could not be further from the truth. Whatever that student believes is possible will be possible. That is why it is important to add a dose of inspiration when giving feedback. Something that will shift their self-image and their capacity to do well. When a student feels unstoppable there's no limit to what they can learn, this then increases the A in BAR.

THE 'A' IS FOR 'ACTION'

Without action, nothing can be done. This is the catalyst to all results, the very effort that is put into a task. Action is affected by three things: intent, intensity and inspiration.

Intent is the reason behind an action, i.e. 'I want to do well in this subject because...' this is the intrinsic motivation. If the intent is strong it creates the foundation for a motivated learner to perform well. This is where I challenge subject teachers to paint a bigger picture of their subject.

A maths teacher is not just teaching maths, she is developing the problem-solving capability so that when students are put in a scenario that requires them to solve a problem they are capable to so do. The world is filled with problems that need solving and maths helps. An English teacher is not just teaching English, he is helping the students develop the ability to use the most powerful tool on the planet – words. Without words we cannot communicate and so if a student can harness the power of words they can deploy any idea.

A music teacher is not just teaching music, she is helping learners tap into a magical force that shapes the human heart. Music is medicine to the soul. When a teacher helps a student express the joys of making music, she is unlocking the wellspring of creativity. The intention behind every subject needs to go beyond grades and educators need to paint that big picture consistently so that learners can stay connected to a powerful intent. Because power follows intention.

Intensity is the second thing that affects action, it is the amount of time, energy and attention given to a task. A half-hearted effort yields no worthwhile result. The more time dedicated to a subject the deeper the knowledge will go. Time is a free currency that every student needs to use wisely to increase their understanding of a subject. Attention is another part of intensity that adds to the force of intensity, you can spend time but if you are not attentive nothing will be assimilated. This is where stickability comes into learning. The ability to stick with a piece of information until understanding has been attained. Attention without assimilation is pointless. Energy is another thing that will propel action. You can spend time and pay attention, but maximum energy needs to be given to the task at hand.

Finally, inspiration is the third force behind action. What is pulling that student forward? This is the magnetic pull that makes them feel a sense of challenge and anticipation, something that sparks their heart for more. If the beliefs are high the action will follow, but belief without action is futile. It is consistent action that gets the results, which is also the final part of the equation.

THE R IS FOR 'RESULT'

This is the outcome of a strong belief system backed by consistent action. If done correctly, the student should see great results. The cause creates the effect and the effect becomes a cause. For example, if the student gets the right kind of feedback that triggers motivation, she then takes the consistent action, when she gets the result her mind stores that and wants to replicate that form of behaviour. It then becomes a cycle. **Feedback** affects **belief** which propels **action**, then a **result** is birthed, this outcome acts as feedback and the cycle continues.

So, you see how feedback can affect not only the student's performance but their self-image. Every subject is connected to a very important factor which is the student. Feedback from one teacher can affect their emotion towards themselves and other subjects. As educators, you have a duty to give feedback that empowers the mind and outlook of the learner. Feedback creates feeling and that feeling needs to be one that empowers the learner to feel that they can achieve and conquer anything in front of them. Let's spark the minds that will create tomorrows change. You get to do that now.

In the following spotlight, Dr Joanne Riordan provides a lens through the eyes of an educational psychologist on the role of feedback and its impact on pupils, teachers and parents.

Specialist Spotlight: The role of feedback

DR JOANNE RIORDAN, EDUCATION PSYCHOLOGIST

Dr Joanne Riordan is an independent educational psychologist and Director of Dr Joanne Ltd. She works with families and schools to help children reach their full potential through assessments, training and direct support with children. Joanne is also a guest lecturer at Royal Holloway, University of London. She completed her doctorate in Educational And Child Psychology at UCL. Previous to her current role, Joanne was a secondary science and psychology teacher and head of Key Stage 3 science, having completed her PGCE at the University of Cambridge. Joanne is passionate about inclusive practices and ensuring every child and young person is given the opportunity to thrive and utilise their strengths.

She lives in Surrey with her husband and three lively children. You can find more information on Facebook @DrJoanneRiordan or her website www.drjoanne.co.uk.

In both my roles as a teacher and educational psychologist, I have provided feedback almost daily to pupils, parents/carers, educators and other external professionals. I've also sought and received feedback from all these groups on many occasions. Yet it is only stopping now to provide this spotlight that I can see how interactional and complex 'feedback' is as a concept. The overarching purpose of feedback within education is conveying a reaction towards a specific behaviour or performance, to improve an individual's or group's future performance. However, once we stop and reflect, we can see that feedback is given for multiple reasons. It is also based on a bi-directional relationship between the feedback 'receiver' and the 'evaluator'.

The way feedback is delivered by educators conveys both our values and current thinking within education and child development. For example, there is a focus currently on moving away from praise and judgement statements (e.g. 'good girl') to giving more encouragement and reflection statements (e.g. 'I really enjoyed reading about this character. What made you want to describe them in this way?'). This is in line with a shift from extrinsic motivation (being motivated by external sources) to trying to foster more intrinsic (internal) motivation.

The themes we choose to provide feedback on also communicate what is important to both ourselves as educators and the curriculum. It is worth reflecting on the feedback you deliver for a day and see if particular patterns emerge. For example, a teacher who highly values a sense of order may find they are giving more feedback on topics such as compliant behaviour and neat handwriting. Those who are proponents of Dweck's work on 'growth mindset', and seeing a skill as something that can be improved, are more likely to see the value in providing improvement points within their feedback.

Feedback is also provided within a relationship between the evaluator and a group or individual. We have societal and cultural norms about feedback. For example, it is commonly assumed that teachers will give feedback to pupils. But it is less expected that pupils will give feedback to teachers, and often feedback in this direction is only viewed as being provided appropriately when sought. We have had past experiences of giving and receiving feedback, and this can unconsciously influence the feedback we give now. In situations where we cannot give feedback to everyone, likely, we are more drawn to giving feedback to certain individuals, based on this history. This is something we need to try and be aware of and reflect on methods to help us deliver feedback more universally.

Once the feedback has been delivered, there are also factors about the receiver that will impact on the feedback. Firstly, does the receiver appreciate that the feedback was meant for them? One area that can be misperceived as not applying to the receiver is group feedback. Individuals who do not agree with the group feedback can be very quick to assume they are part of a minority to whom it does not apply. Also, certain individuals, such as those with social communication difficulties such as autism spectrum disorder, can find it hard to realise that group information also includes them, and therefore may not take it on board. Other factors that impact on whether the message was received include whether the receiver is attending to the feedback and their ability to access the language used in the feedback.

There are certain instances where even if the evaluator provided the feedback in a way that it could be received, it may still be rejected. Firstly, it depends on whether the receiver trust and values both the feedback itself and the particular evaluator, and this often depends on the relationship between the two parties and norms we have about how we expect feedback to be given. Secondly, it depends on how safe or threatening the feedback is to us. Feedback given privately tends to be safer than that given in front of a group. Positive and neutral feedback tends to be safer than negative feedback. In contrast, negative feedback about an area we value, without constructively informing us how to improve, is the riskiest. Feedback which is viewed as unsafe can lead to an emotional reaction, that means we are not able to rationally take on board the feedback.

So, this naturally leads me on to reflecting on what then is the most effective way of delivering feedback. I think we need to go a step back before we even consider any feedback and reflect on the values of the system we are in and ourselves as evaluators. Is there a whole-school ethos that gives value to feedback? Using 'growth mindset' can be a good framework for highlighting to all members of the school community that we are all constantly learning in all domains and can all improve together. We then need to reflect on why we are giving feedback to others. Why are you choosing the specific themes you feedback on? Why are you choosing to give feedback to that specific individual and in that moment also? We also need to reflect on our relationship with the receiver of the feedback. We should ensure that the receiver trusts that we will give feedback fairly and trusts that we know this area. The feedback needs to be delivered at a time that the individual can attend to and reflect on that feedback, which may differ between receivers. Finally, it is about ensuring that feedback is as non-threatening as possible. If negative feedback is provided, then we should ensure we also communicate clearly how the individual can improve. This conveys the message that we believe that they can improve and that this is not merely a criticism.

In this way, feedback is not just about helping others to make progress. It is also a tool for conveying our values and for developing our relationships with others.

Teacher Spotlight: Delivering feedback in the secondary classroom

AMY SEARLE, GEOGRAPHY TEACHER AND CURRICULUM COORDINATOR

Amy is a geography teacher at Burford School, Oxfordshire, and is currently in her seventh year of teaching. She has a passion for teaching and learning and has used this energy to complete an MA in Teaching Studies at the University of Birmingham. In addition to teaching geography, Amy has recently taken on an exciting new role as the whole school curriculum coordinator: research and development lead. You can find her tweeting as @MissASearle

For each year group, we have a set of common assessment tasks to ensure consistency in assessment and feedback. The common assessment tasks are the key stones of each topic and underpin the development of geographical knowledge and skills. The tasks take three forms: topic tests, feedback grids and extended assessments. As an example, at Key Stage 3, there are typically two topic tests and two feedback grids per topic, depending on length, with three extended assessments per year. Feedback is delivered through a combination of individual and whole-class feedback.

TOPIC TESTS

Topic tests are 10-20 question quizzes used to assess students' geographical knowledge and understanding of topics studied, as well as to support retrieval practice.

At Key Stage 4 and Key Stage 5, students complete weekly quizzes built on GCSEpod and Seneca Learn respectively. These quizzes are completed out of lesson time, with dedicated time the following lesson for teacher-led feedback. Electronic quizzing makes it easy to identify common misconceptions. When looking at the performance summary in GCSEpod, the question that students answered best/worst is automatically highlighted (see figure 1) as well as an average score for each question. A similar performance summary is provided by Seneca Learn. Whilst it is important to note that not every child will have the same misconceptions, the summary provides a useful signpost towards future areas of discussion. A one-slide summary can then be produced to support the teacher-led discussions that follow and ensure that we feedforward to address any misconceptions that students may have, helping to close the feedback loop. This information can also be used to evaluate and recommend future adjustments to schemes of learning. Below is a screenshot of a performance summary from a GCSEpod quiz.

Most correct answers:	Most incorrect answers:
Q4 (76%)	Q5 (38%)

At Key Stage 3, our topic tests had always been completed in class with questions projected onto the screen and students answering them on paper. These were then peer-assessed as a class and overall scores collected, meaning that the information shared with the teacher could be limited beyond the total score.

As such, our Key Stage 3 topic tests have moved online. The quizzes have been written on Microsoft Forms, which means that faster, deeper teacher analysis can occur due to the rich data being electronically gathered. As with the Key Stage 4 and Key Stage 5 provision, by completing the quizzes at home future lesson time can be better using whole-class feedback to show students how to make improvements, address misconceptions and feedforward into future learning. Topics or skills that students found difficult are also targeted in future in-class retrieval starters too.

FEEDBACK GRIDS

It goes without saying that we cannot and do not mark every piece of work. Instead, we focus on key stones – specific pieces of work that we believe are fundamental to progress in each topic and, indeed, in a student's overall geographical learning journey. The tasks will vary by year group and by topic: a Year 7 student may draw and describe a climate graph, a Year 9 student may create a storyboard explaining the formation of a stump, whilst a Year 12 student may write a response to a 12-mark question but each task has been identified as a key stone within the learning. These tasks all have clear, student-friendly success criteria shared at the start of the task, and feedback is provided using a feedback grid.

The feedback grid structure varies slightly between key stages but the principles remain the same (see figures 2 and 3 for Key Stage 3 and Key Stage 5 examples respectively). After completing the task, the student gives a personal effort score from 1-4 whilst the peer assesses the work against the student-friendly success criteria, before providing a 'strength' and an 'action' for the student. Exemplar 'strengths' and 'actions' are modelled to students to ensure high-quality feedback is provided. In this way, the peer assessment can also be used by the original student to support self-reflection of their own work (Enser, 2019).

Tropical rainforest climate graph feedback		
Name: Effort self review: 1 2 3 4	**Peer reviewer:**	Strengths: what have they done well? ☺
Success criteria: ☐ Climate graph accurately drawn. ☐ Bars coloured blue and line coloured red. ☐ Pattern of the graph is described. ☐ Facts (evidence) used to back up points.		Action: what could they do to improve?
Students response to actions: ☐ Tick this box if action completed on original work Date actioned: _____		Teacher feedback: Effort score: 1 2 3 4 (best)

The above shows an example of a feedback grid for part of a Year 7 geography 'ecosystems' topic.

The teacher feedback that follows is granular, meaning it is task-specific so the student can identify their successes in the task and feed this forward into future learning. The feedback must be transferable to future tasks, so whilst being task-specific it must also support the development of transferable skills. In addition, there is a focus on the student's effort rather than their attainment.

At Key Stage 4 and Key Stage 5, feedback grids are used to review a student's response to an exam question. The strengths and target are shared with the student, and their 'action' is to conduct these improvements for this specific question, following whole-class discussions and modelling. In this way, students can see how the suggested improvements can be applied across different topic areas, rather than being unique to the individual question. The feedback grid also helps students to recognises the value in redrafting and improving their work, rather than seeing a piece of work as a finished product. Figure 3 shows an example of a completed feedback grid for a Year 12 student's exam question.

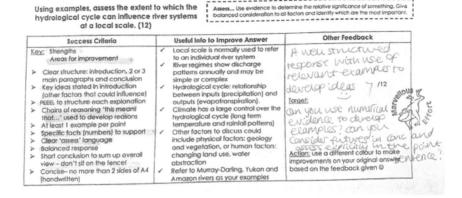

The above is an example of a feedback grid for a Year 12 exam question in 'The Water Cycle and Water Security' topic in Edexcel A Level geography.

EXTENDED ASSESSMENTS

Feedback following a formal extended assessment occurs in a similar format to the feedback grids – strengths, actions and targets. This consistency increases the usefulness and usability of the feedback for the students. Students will first review their own learning by using the success criteria to give themselves a strength, action and effort score, before submitting the work to their teacher. The teacher then uses a combination of whole class and individualised feedback; strengths are summarised individually for each student, and they are then assigned a numbered action and target. The action is always task-specific, whilst the target shows students where this improvement fits into their jigsaw of geographical learning overall. These actions and targets are discussed and modelled in-lesson, giving students time to make granular improvements to their current piece of work whilst also making connections and building blocks to support their future learning and progress in geography.

Following an assessment on the impacts of the 2011 Tohoku tsunami, a student's action could be to 'explain the wider impacts of the tsunami nationally and globally' if they had only included localised impacts in their writing. Completing this action is modelled to the class, and students would be signposted to the source of this information to ensure they can access this meaningfully. Their target would be 'to consider impacts at a range of spatial scales' so that in future writing they consider local, national and global impacts from the get-go. This format exemplifies the importance of feedback to feedforward – using feedback in the classroom to maximise progress.

Key takeaways

- Feedback is everywhere and plays a pivotal role in learning about ourselves and shaping how others perceive themselves.
- Feedback has the primary purpose of addressing the understanding gap based on how someone has performed relative to the anticipated goals.
- Feedback can be a fundamental cog in driving one of the wheels of our education but equally one of the most variable in its effectiveness for teachers, pupils, and parents.
- The variability in its effectiveness in recent times can be attributed to the degree to which the word feedback has been interpreted.
- Teachers provide pupils with feedback all the time, but it is the acting on the feedback that contributes to pupil learning.
- Creating the right conditions where pupils, teachers and parents want to receive, seek out, use, and give feedback is important to ensure that it is effective and efficient at supporting learning.

Chapter reflections

Use the space below to reflect on your own experiences of feedback.

Chapter 1 references

Ames, C. (1992) 'Classrooms: Goals, structures, and student motivation', *Journal of Educational Psychology* 84 (3) pp. 261–271.

Archer, J. C. (2010) 'State of the science in health professional education: effective feedback', *Medical Education* 44 pp. 101-108.

Boud, D. and Molloy, E. (2013) 'Decision-making for feedback' in D. Boud and E. Molloy (eds.) *Feedback in Higher and Professional Education*. London: Routledge, pp. 202-217.

Butler, D. L. and Winne, P. H. (1995) 'Feedback and Self-Regulated Learning: A Theoretical Synthesis', *Review of Educational Research* 65 (3) pp. 245-281.

Chappuis, J. (2012) 'How Am I Doing?', *Feedback for Learning* 70 (1) pp. 36-41.

Corbett, A. T. and Anderson, J. R. (2001) 'Locus of Feedback Control in Computer-Based Tutoring: Impact on Learning Rate, Achievement and Attitudes' In J. Jacko, A. Sears, M. Beaudouin-Lafon and R. Jacob (eds.) *Proceedings of ACM CHI'2001 Conference on Human Factors in Computing Systems*, pp. 245-252. New York: ACM Press.

Dehaene, S. (2019) *How We Learn*. London: Penguin.

Didau, D. (2016) 'Workload Challenge: Marking', *Learning Spy* [Online] 26 March. Retrieved from: www.bit.ly/3kmla8A

Didau, D. (2014) 'Getting feedback right part 3: How can we increase pupils' effort?', *The Learning Spy* [Online] 19 March. Retrieved from: www.bit.ly/3lubzOq

Enser, M. (2019) *Making Every Geography Lesson Count*. Carmarthen: Crown House.

Hattie, J. (2009) *Visible Learning: A synthesis of over 800 meta-analyses relating to achievement*. London: Routledge.

Hattie, J. and Timperley, H. (2007) 'The Power of Feedback', *Review of Educational Research* 77 (1) pp. 81-112.

Independent Teacher Workload Review Group (2016) 'Eliminating unnecessary workload around marking'. Retrieved from: www.bit.ly/3pfmy0J

Kostons, D., van Gog, T. and Paas, F. (2012) 'Training self-assessment and task-selection skills: A cognitive approach to improving self-regulated learning', *Learning and Instruction* 22 (2) pp. 121-132.

Kulhavy, R. W. and Anderson, R. C. (1972) 'Delay-retention effect with multiple-choice tests', *Journal of Educational Psychology* 63 (5) pp. 505-512.

Lysakowski, R. S. and Walberg, H. J. (1982) 'Instructional effects of cues, participation, and corrective feedback: A quantitative synthesis', *American Educational Research Journal* 19 (4) pp. 559-578.

Mathan, S. A. and Koedinger, K. R. (2002) 'An empirical assessment of comprehension fostering features in an intelligent tutoring system' In S. A. Cerri, G. Gouarderes and F. Paraguacu (eds.), Intelligent Tutoring Systems, 6th International Conference, ITS2002 (Vol. 2363, pp. 330–343). New York: Springer-Verlag.

Miser, W. F. (no date) 'Giving Effective Feedback'. Retrieved from: www.bit.ly/36lHhqO

Mutch, A. (2003) 'Exploring the Practice of Feedback to Students', *Active Learning in Higher Education* 4 (1) pp. 24-38.

Ofsted (2018) 'Ofsted inspection – clarification for schools'. Retrieved from: www.bit.ly/377F3M4

Orwell, J. (2006) 'Feedback on learning achievement: Rhetoric and reality', *Teaching in Higher Education* 11 (4) pp. 441-456.

Schroth, M. L. (1992) 'The effects of delay of feedback on a delayed concept formation transfer task', *Contemporary Educational Psychology* 17 (1) pp. 78-82.

Schunk, D. H. and Ertmer, P. A. (2000) 'Self-regulation and academic learning: Self-efficacy enhancing interventions', In M. Boekaerts, P. R. Pintrich and M. Zeidner (eds) *Handbook of self-regulation* (p. 631–649). Academic Press.

Shute, V. J. (2007) 'Focus on Formative Feedback', *Educational Testing Service*.

Soderstrom, N. C. and Bjork, R. A. (2014) 'Learning Versus Performance: An Integrative review', *Perspectives on Psychological Science* 10 (2) pp. 176-199.

Stone, D. and Heen, S. (2014) *Thanks for the Feedback: The Science and Art of Receiving Feedback Well*. London: Penguin.

Strauss, S., Ziv, M. and Stein, A. (2002) 'Teaching as a Natural Cognition and Its Relations to Preschoolers' Developing Theory of Mind', *Cognitive Development* 17, pp. 1473-1487.

Veloski, J., Boex, J. R., Grasberger, M. J., Evans, A. and Wolfson, D. B. (2006) 'Systematic review of the literature on assessment, feedback and physicians' clinical performance: BEME Guide No. 7', *Medical Teacher* 28 (2) pp. 117-128.

Walker, M., Worth, J., Van den Brande, J. and National Foundation for Educational Research (2019) 'Teacher workload survey 2019: Research report'. London: The Stationery Office.

Wiliam, D. (2011) *Embedded Formative Assessment*. Bloomington, IN: Solution Tree Press.

Zimmerman, B. J. (2010) 'Becoming a Self-Regulated Learner: An Overview', *Theory into Practice* 41 (2).

Zimmerman, B. J. (2000) 'Attaining self-regulation: A social cognitive perspective' In M. Boekaerts, P. R. Pintrich and M. Zeidner (eds.) *Handbook of self-regulation* (p. 13–39). Academic Press.

2

FEEDBACK TO PUPILS: HOW CAN FEEDBACK SUPPORT PUPILS TO FEEDFORWARD?

'The first fundamental principle of effective classroom feedback is that feedback should be more work for the recipient than the donor.' – Dylan Wiliam

Chapter checklist

✓ Spend time priming pupils to receive your feedback
✓ Explicitly teach pupils about the role of feedback in their learning
✓ Feedback is just as important for teachers as it is for pupils
✓ Actively involve pupils in the learning journey

✓ Explicitly link the feedback to the original intentions of the task
✓ Create opportunities for pupils to self and peer assess to promote active engagement
✓ Reduce feedback that focuses on 'praise and reward'
✓ Provide feedback on the merits of the work, not the pupil
✓ Create a culture where the values of feedback are instilled in every pupil

2.1 Priming pupils for feedback

From our exploration of the concept of feedback in chapter 1, we concluded that providing feedback is powerful but can equally be problematic. The more problematic it becomes, the degree to which it is effective in supporting learning diminishes. Therefore, as we have already established, providing feedback is a challenge and one that needs to be sustainable for teachers and pupils. It is our responsibility as teachers to create and cultivate the right conditions for pupils to receive feedback. If we want our feedback to be effective, we need to prime pupils to want to receive the feedback we provide to them. So, how can we do this?

1. Curriculum coherence
2. Establishing and embedding the art of subject success
3. Clarity of learning intentions
4. Creating a receptive culture

First and foremost, for feedback to provide a meaningful contribution to the learning process, what we teach and how we teach it needs to be well thought out. This is where, as teachers, we should carefully plan what we want pupils to learn and what we expect success will look like when they have learnt about the concept or process they are being taught. This is something Mary Myatt discusses in her book *The Curriculum: Gallimaufry to coherence*: 'planning is critical and it is fundamental in providing the structure and architecture for pupils' learning.' Therefore, when it comes to priming pupils for feedback, teachers must decide in the first instance what they are going to teach and how they are going to carefully construct the activities that pupils will undertake to allow pupils to think hard and then demonstrate their thinking.

Co-constructing schemes of work with colleagues at departmental meetings can be effective in building a collaborative discussion on the best approaches to explaining concepts and processes. The curriculum needs coherence to make it meaningful to both teachers and pupils. It is important to declutter and create sequences of lessons that are underpinned by a clear rationale that is understood by all teachers in the department. If we do not create coherence it can lead to a cluttered curriculum that creates strands of knowledge that are not threaded together; a bit like a patchwork quilt that has become threadbare. The construction of the curriculum and the subsequent tasks to demonstrate learning are important in creating the foundations for feedback to have a purpose for both the pupil and the teacher.

When we have established a curriculum with coherence it is then important to establish what success will look like based on the learning intentions. This is because I firmly believe our role as teachers is to illuminate the key ingredients to success so that pupils have in mind 'a concept of quality roughly similar to that held by the teacher' (Sadler, 1989). At the same time, we want to anticipate the potential misconceptions that pupils have in our subject. Planning for these, creating misconception maps to accompany schemes of work during departmental CPD time can support effective planning and prime pupils before moving from guided to independent practice. Taking the time to consider these and how we can overcome them is in my opinion an important use of our time. Anticipating these pupils errors is something Rosenshine indicated were one of the characteristics of the most effective teachers, 'one characteristic of effective teachers is their ability to anticipate students' errors and warn them about possible errors some of them are likely to make.' Sharing the key elements to success can come in several forms.

The first is feedback related to deepening understanding of the disciplinary traits connected to being successful in the subject. For example, what it means to be a successful geographer, historian or mathematician. Sharing this criterion with pupils regularly by showing them how to be successful in your subject can help them to understand their role and free up working memory and aid transferability to different tasks over time. Doing this helps to reduce the anxiety pupils can feel and creates structure. We can set and stress pupil attention by levering the filter and following mechanisms of our attention. Something we discussed in chapter 1. For example, this might include the following guidance:

- In history, great historians draw together and analyse a range of sources.
- In maths, mathematicians remember to include their working out to demonstrate how they arrived at their outcome.
- In geography, geographers construct graphs using a pencil, labelling their axes and a clear title.
- In English, a good writer proofreads what they have written to check for spelling and punctuation accuracy.
- In science, an excellent scientist will be able to critique methods and data they are presented with, identifying strengths, weaknesses and how to develop the line of enquiry further.
- In art, a good artist will consider the formal elements of line, colour and pattern when drawing.
- In music, a good musician will use composition techniques through score writing or real-time recording to convey their chosen emotion.
- In religious education, a good philosopher will always consider both sides of the argument.
- In computer science, when writing code, an efficient programmer will first visualise a program before creating detailed algorithms to solve specific problems.

These transferable strategies for how to be successful in a subject could be displayed in the classroom, in their school planners or the front of their exercise books. Regular reference back to these strategies throughout the academic year will be important in developing their automaticity, along with modelling how these can be applied to a specific task. The second type of success criteria is related to how the pupil can be successful at the necessary processes related to the task. If this is well prepared and clearly communicated to pupils before completing the task, this can help to reduce cognitive load and free up their working memory. A process-related success criterion for a specific subject might include the following:

- Extract data from the graph to support your point (maths/geography).
- Provide a balanced response which includes the views from at least four different stakeholders (geography/English).

- Try to incorporate shading into your drawing (art).
- Remember to include evidence of the process you took for working out the sum (maths).

This subject targeted success criteria can support pupils in developing automaticity in our subjects by reducing the cognitive load associated with explicit reference to the transferable processes that pupil's need to demonstrate. The more this is referenced through orienteering their attention, the greater this will become automatic and the less repetitive feedback required. This will, in turn, free up space for pupils to focus their attention on deepening their understanding of the subject. To develop this common language, provide pupils with guides to support their understanding of what it means to be a geographer, historian, mathematician, scientist and so on.

Finally, when priming pupils for feedback creating and embedding a receptive culture – one of the key principles outlined in chapter 1 – so that it prepares pupils to appreciate its value and want to willingly receive feedback.

1. Familiarise your pupils with the process of how their feedback will be provided and the rationale for this format.
2. Exemplify the importance of and model how feedback can contribute to improving learning.
3. Normalise the different process of receiving feedback regularly so that it becomes something that is part of the lesson.
4. Clarify the reasons why improving work based on feedback can support improvement in understanding of the subject in the longer term.

In the next spotlight, primary school teacher Emily Weston shares how she approaches feedback in the classroom.

Teacher Spotlight: A reflection on feedback

EMILY WESTON, TRANSITION TEACHER

Emily has been teaching for seven years. For the first six years, she taught primary school – predominantly Year 6 – as well as taking on the role of reading lead within the school. Recently, she has made the transition to secondary, taking on the role of transition teacher within a newly-opened school in Swindon. You can find her tweeting as @primaryteachew

Marking and feedback is something teachers have done since the profession began, yet recently there has been so much discussion, focus and research based on feedback and marking to discern what works best for the little people we work with. Once upon a time, we would be expected to complete marking which felt like almost as much work as the child had done. At the time, it felt as though we were giving them really valuable feedback; writing what went well and what needs improving will surely help children improve, right? More recently though, we have seen the benefits of live marking within the lesson and reducing the time we spend writing in books after the lesson. This is particularly true for younger children in the primary phase; reading feedback, which they may not independently understand, is never going to be as valuable as live feedback.

At a school I worked at, we were expected to 'in-depth mark' extended pieces of writing twice a week: one topic and one writing. For this, we had to mark missing or incorrect punctuation, underline and correct spellings and also use a variety of symbols to denote paragraphs, phrases that didn't make sense and misconceptions or mistakes made in the writing. For a class of 35 children, this would take hours, and I am sure you're not surprised to hear that it had little impact on the children. It was too much for them to focus on. Yes, they could correct a few spellings or put a comma where a missed piece of punctuation was signalled, but did they understand why? And this is what I think is so important: children knowing the 'why' of their reflections and corrections. It isn't worth the hours of work written marking can so often be when the understanding hasn't developed. This is why live marking is so brilliant for primary.

Firstly, we can focus on misconceptions there and then, instead of a written comment at the end of a lesson where a gap of learning will then occur between the learning and reflection. Reiterating in the lesson will help with the retention of understanding. Live marking also works particularly well for quieter children in this way, who might not share in discussion or want to ask for help. Secondly, by live marking, you can see not only when an individual has misconceptions, but also a small group or, in some cases, the class. Because of this, my TA and I started using morning interventions in a much more interactive (and at risk of using the word too many times) and reactive way. Instead of leaving straight after the input for group work, we would wait five minutes to discern which children might need some adult input. It's important to remember, too, that different children might find their misconceptions lie in different topics. A child who finds fractions tricky may well excel when it comes to cubed numbers. By selecting children during live marking that could benefit from additional modelling and adult input you can target their learning. As mentioned previously, if it is the majority of the class you can pause and re-teach the concept. Not all feedback has to be individualised!

Finally, the reduction of marking workload increases the ability to manage your work/life balance. Now, not every evening is loaded with marking, which means you can work towards being even more of an impact within the classroom.

2.2 Verbal 'live' feedback

Despite the research and the myth-busting, teachers still spend hours each week providing written comments on pupil's books. This was illustrated from the results generated by Teacher Tapp where teachers still spend an average of three to eight hours a week marking work. All too often, as we discussed in chapter 1, this marking is a waste of time and has minimal impact on pupil's learning. However, it has a significant impact on teacher time. Teacher's time is precious and we should look to create systems that allow teachers time to be optimised that will contribute towards boosting learning. One way to reduce this burden is through regular verbal feedback.

In 2019, in the UCL Verbal Feedback Project with Ross McGill, one teacher defined verbal feedback as: 'Verbal feedback involves teachers engaging and interacting more with their students on both a one-to-one and whole class level. It allows teachers to give and students to receive immediate feedback that is meaningful. It allows teachers to identify, quickly, common misconceptions either by circulating or through the one-to-one conversations had. These misconceptions can then be addressed as a class so that all students can continue making progress.'

Verbal feedback allows for 'live' in the moment guidance to pupils to steer them in the direction towards success. It can reveal any of the underlining misconceptions that they may still have and reduce the potential to have to pick up these points after the work has been completed. There are several ways that we can implement a verbal feedback approach in our classrooms. Firstly, we can circulate the room and check their work. When circulating the room, you can offer corrective feedback which can be defined as, 'responses to learners utterances containing an error' (Ellis et al, 2006). When you identify something, use this opportunity to 'check their understanding' through the 'quiet and guide' method by asking them to clarify a point that they have made.

'Tom, can you give me a specific example from the source for that point you have just made...?'

'Tom, remember to include a quote to support the point you have just made.'

'Tom, can you re-read that sentence to me.'

This allows you to steer Tom back on track to reduce any potential procedural errors becoming embedded in his work. It will take longer to undue these procedural errors if feedback is delayed when the advice is instead provided in the following lesson. This verbal feedback can be reinforced through reference back to the success criteria and allows pupils to engage in self-regulation to review the desired learning intentions. When re-directing pupils through this feedback it would be beneficial to get Tom to repeat your advice back to you before you move away. This allows you to check that Tom has understood the feedback he has received and involve them in the process. This exchange of feedback provides opportunities for you to build relationships with pupils through these short coaching conversations.

Once you are happy with their response, you can return after a few minutes to check that they have taken in your advice. Taking the time to return and check on their progress also reinforces to the pupil your commitment to the feedback process. In chapter 1, we discussed the importance of establishing a receptive culture where pupils want to embrace the feedback we share. If we don't return to check this could suggest the initial feedback provided was not important, or to be acted upon. These regular 'quiet and guide' opportunities reflect what Barak Rosenshine (2012) indicated was one of the hallmarks of the more effective teachers who, 'check of student understanding: checking for student understanding at each point can help students learn the material with fewer errors'.

Secondly, teachers can create opportunities for more detailed one to one verbal 'feedback bites' during the lesson. When circulating the room, you may notice that a pupil needs further direction to dispel misconceptions and put them back on the track to success. You call that student over to your desk to provide this feedback. This allows you to spend time providing more in-depth feedback. During a lesson, you might use this option to give this feedback to a handful of pupils who need that further support to reach the learning intention.

Regardless of the way in which the feedback is given during the lesson, while circulating or in a more detailed way at your desk, asking lots of questions is an important part of the feedback process. When teachers ask questions, this provides an opportunity to establish current knowledge based on how well the material has been learnt (Rosenshine, 2012). The questions we ask pupils allows us to probe their understanding and provide feedback based on their responses. Questioning is a dominant feature of our classrooms and as Filippone indicated in 1998, one of the most effective tools to stimulate thinking in the classroom.

The effectiveness of the questions you ask will be determined by its ability to invoke the right emotions and thoughts. To quote Albert Einstein in the 2002 book *Physique, philosophie, politique*: 'If I had an hour to solve a problem, and my life depended on the solution, I would spend the first 55 minutes determining the proper question to ask... for once I know the proper question, I could solve the problem in less than five minutes.'

The development of good questions requires careful thought and planning. Wilen and Clegg (1986) indicated several key principles teachers should consider when using questioning in the classroom:

- Phrase the question clearly.
- Ask questions of primarily an academic nature.
- Allow three or five seconds of wait time after asking a question before requesting a student's response, particularly when high-cognitive level questions are asked.
- Encourage students to respond in some way to each question asked.
- Elicit a high percentage of correct responses from students and assist with incorrect responses.
- Probe students' responses to have them clarify ideas, support a point of view or extend their thinking.

In an early conducted study by Wragg (1993) illustrated that the type of questions teachers ask fall into three main types:

1. Management related: 'How many of you haven't finished the piece of work?'
2. Information recall: 'How many wives did Henry VIII have?'
3. Higher order: 'Why do you think Shakespeare portrayed...?'

In the study, Wragg found that the most common questions asked were management related whereas the last commonly asked questions were higher order. This was also seen in Pate and Bremer's research findings based on a study of 190 teachers in US elementary schools. If we are to maximise the benefit of using questions to gather feedback, we should aim to ask a range of question types from the information recall to promote retrieval practice and the higher order to encourage greater development of answers.

Questioning strategy 1 – the extender: tell me more...

One way of gathering further feedback is to ask questions that encourage pupils to develop their response. There is a tendency for pupils to give a short response that often lacks depth. Ask pupils to extend their initial response to help unravel their understanding. An example of how this can be achieved is shown by the question stems below.

'Can you give me an example...?'

'What do you mean...?'

'Can you develop this further...?'

'Expand on this by...?'

'Why did you choose this...?'

'What evidence supports your point...?'

Using these probing questions can be powerful in developing a deeper understanding of pupil knowledge. It allows pupils to elaborate on what they have learnt and develop further connections to previous learning in their long-term memory. Whilst these high-order questions help move beyond knowledge recall, we should be mindful that low-level cognitive questions still have a place in the classroom to support the rehearsal of knowledge and develop automaticity. This will support the responses to high-level cognitive questions. In particular, the use of this more scaffolded approach can be beneficial for lower ability pupils who may need guided practice to unravel their understanding. We want to avoid the one-word response which can lead to 'cognitively restricting rituals' (Alexander, 2006). We must challenge all pupils to expand on our responses and not just accept closed responses because this does our pupils a disservice.

Questioning strategy 2 – the unveiling: tell me something...

There have been many times in the early stages of my career where the thought of questioning pupils to gauge their understanding was quite daunting. The standard response for many pupils was 'I don't know'. I suspect I haven't been the only one and, at this point, I would move on to another pupil because I did not want to delve deeper into the reasons why they didn't know. The problem with this, as we discussed in chapter 1, is that pupils would rather choose to be lazy. By saying I don't know gives them an easy way out of not having to think about providing a response and reduce the feat of potentially getting it wrong. This is where building a receptive culture where pupils feel that they can contribute publicly in front of their peers without the fear of retribution is important. This will take time to establish but perseverance in not accepting the default 'I don't know' response will mean you can gather feedback to check their understanding.

Questioning strategy 3 – the chain: build on it...

There will be times when you want to use questioning to build on a specific concept or process by involving several pupils. Here is an example of a script where the teacher is using questioning to build on and layer understanding of Hitler's rise to power.

Teacher: What were the main reasons for Hitler's rise to power from 1929-1933?

Student A: Uh, propaganda sir.

Teacher: Thanks Student A I'm going to be coming back to you so pay attention to the next answers. Who agrees that propaganda was one of the main reasons for Hitler's rise to power?

Teacher: Student B, why do you agree with that in a full sentence please?

Student B: I agree because he had his Minister for Propaganda, Josef Goebbels, write speeches for him and create his Hitler over Germany campaign which made him more popular.

Teacher: Excellent, who can add to that for me? (brief pause) Student C!

Student C: They also had the work and bread scheme to appeal to the working classes who didn't have jobs at the time.

Teacher: Excellent, student C, thank you. Now, student A, back to you. Improve your initial answer using what we've heard from the rest of the room. Remember, I want full sentences here.

Student A: Um. Hitler was able to come to power because he used propaganda such as the Hitler over Germany campaign and the work and bread posters to appeal to the working classes.

Teacher: And who organised a lot of this for Hitler according to student B?

Student A: Josef Goebbels, wasn't it?

Teacher: Excellent! Much better answer write that down in your book for me and I'll come and check it in a minute.

Of course, it does not matter how well we plan our questions, we need to ensure we create the conditions where our pupils want to respond. There will be some pupils who will inevitably want to respond to our questions, the keen bean! On the other hand, we will have pupils who will want to hide and not voice their thoughts. There are several ways we can work to overcome these differences:

1. Establish a 'no hands' up approach to signal that you will choose someone to answer a question
2. When pupils are asked to answer a question create a climate where answering questions provide a confidence boost and not an embarrassing moment
3. Give pupils 'wait time' to allow them to process the question you have asked.

2.3 Whole class feedback

When providing feedback, it should be more work for the pupil and not for you as the teacher. The repetitive comments repeated across a whole set of books should be a marking approach of the past. It wastes teachers time and does not have the desired impact on feeding pupils forward, as well as being a dispiriting process. A more streamlined process to reduce the time spent writing the same comments and diluting the focus on common misconceptions and areas for improvement, whole class feedback is an effective approach. As with any feedback strategy, the challenge is how whole class feedback is implemented. There is the danger it might not have the desired impact. When using whole class feedback, I would advocate the following principles illustrated in the following graphic organiser, created kindly by David Goodwin. The core focus here on improving the pupil, not just the work.

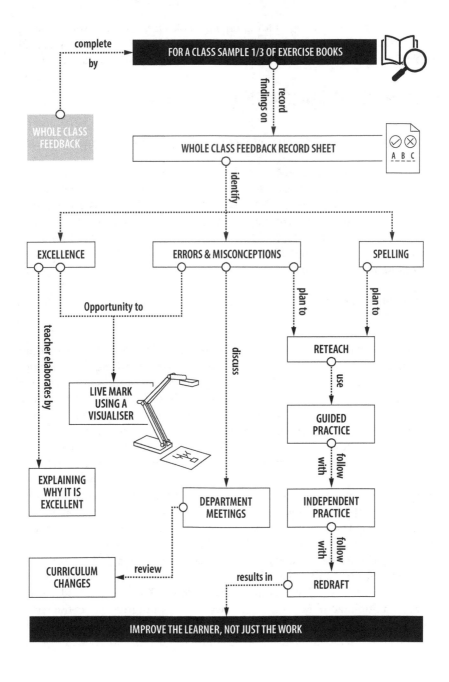

In considering these principles for applying whole class feedback the following two spotlights, Greg Thornton and Neil Almond share how they use WCF (whole class feedback) in the context of primary and secondary classrooms.

Teacher Spotlight: WCF case study

GREG THORNTON, HISTORY SUBJECT LEADER AT MEOLS COP HIGH SCHOOL

Greg Thornton is a teacher and head of history, currently working at a Research School. He currently supports his schools NQT programme, T&L training whilst providing CPD through the EEF & Research School Network. He is a chartered teacher who is interested in curriculum, feedback and the application of cognitive science into history pedagogy. Greg writes and shares resources on his blog mrthorntonteach.com and is currently curating 'History How To', a collaborative project between history practitioners.

You can find him tweeting as @MrThorntonTeach

As a new head of department in 2016, I had inherited a messy and overwhelming marking and feedback policy which focused on triple marking, teacher-pupil dialogue and the expectation that every page 'had something written on'. As a history teacher, this was time invasive; I could spend three-plus hours making each classes books and still not really grasp what the issues were in my class. Indeed, at the bottom of 20+ paragraphs essays, I would write comments such as, 'you need to link back to the question more consistently' or 'refer to the provenance of the source', without really spending time on re-teaching this to the class. Instead, the 'DIRT' time in the next lesson would involve students all doing the same things independently and me pottering around giving individual feedback rather than dealing with the issues as a whole class. I'll also admit that as a soon to be father, there was considerable pressure to reduce my workload and this was the final push I needed to try something different.

One night, I decided to make a basic sheet of four boxes (What Went Well, Even Better If, SPaG and To Do) that I scrawled notes on for each class. The aim of this was to get a better 'big picture' of each class as I felt sometimes I was too 'micro' and not 'macro' enough in my view of class progress. Over the spring term, this evolved into a 'crib' sheet which I trialled with a GCSE class, with the focus on no written comments in books and solely using whole class feedback.

History Marking Crib Sheet		Date:	Class	
Praise	Feedback		Literacy Key Terms SPaG	
			Activities	
Even Better If				
Presentation	Polaroid Moments			

Despite the misgivings from some of my students who missed the writing in their books, the trial was a success, with no negative impact on student progress. Importantly, my focus had shifted from marking for the sake of it to a becoming a more responsive teacher who was more in tune with student's progress and aware of the actions I needed to take to help them. In hindsight, I began to focus on what Dylan Wiliam says as 'improve the pupil, not just the work', as both my feedback lessons and subsequent planning began to focus closing gaps, moving students on and tackling misconceptions.

I will acknowledge that whilst it only takes 30 minutes or less to go through books, I have begun to spend a little more time on planning 'feedback' lessons based on the WCF sheet, which I feel is justified. The feedback lessons I create are more in-tuned to the needs of the class than ever.

Furthermore, during the trial my line manager shared the recently released EEF 'A Marked Improvement' Report, the findings of Hattie and Joe Kirby's blog post 'Marking is a hornet', which confirmed that I was heading down the right path. In the years since, the work of Wiliam, Christodoulou and Fletcher-Wood have all contributed to the honing of our feedback policy and it has been pleasing to see its growth in the education world.

Having trialled WCF for a term, I presented my findings to the senior leadership team who were highly supportive of the new approach, which I likened to a 'tuning fork' as it allowed me to take a snapshot of where students were at and highlighted the tweaks I needed to make to keep them on track. With this support, we rolled out the new Whole Class Feedback policy across the history department in September 2016 and it has stayed this way since.

Whole class feedback has transformed our department, changing the way we mark, work and plan.

Assessment feedback

EQ: Did the Normans bring a *'truckload of trouble'* to England?					Total /40
Success criteria	1	2	3	4	Complete two of the following actions
Relevant The best answers will use relevant and accurate knowledge related to the topic and question throughout their essay					Go back through your essay and correct any inaccuracies that your teacher has identified.
Specific The best answers will use specific knowledge throughout their answer, using key terms, dates, statistics and names.					Go back through your essay and add any specific knowledge missing from your answer, e.g. *500 Motte and Bailey Castles were built, the Harrying of the North, Domesday Book or Archbishop Stigand.*
Range and scope The best answers will consider a wide range of evidence from the topics to support their points, to agree or disagree					Go back through your essay and add another reason you agree or disagree with Schama's view, *for example add about the changes to slaves or women, or discuss the rebellions caused by Norman rule.*
Balance The best answers provide a balanced answer the question, with paragraphs that agree and disagree with Schama's interpretation.					Go back through your essay and add another paragraph to agree or disagree with Schama's view that the Normans brought a 'truckload of trouble' to England, e.g. *'On the other hand, there is evidence to suggest the Normans had a positive impact on England as....'*
Conclusion The best answers end with a detailed conclusion that justifies their opinion on where they are or disagree with Schama.					Add or redraft your conclusion to add more detail to explain the reasoning for your opinion, e.g. *'I _____ with Schama's interpretation of the Norman impact of England as........'*
Change and Continuity The best answers provided a range of examples to explain the changes made by the Normans to England. This includes both positive and negative changes to the country.					Go back through your essay and look for any further examples of the changes the Normans made which you could use to support your points, e.g. *'A further change to the life of peasants was that was that with the rising taxes, many Freeman had to become Villeins as...'*
Interpretation The best answers refer to Schama's interpretation throughout the answer, picking quotes to support or contradict.					Go back through your essay and add a quote to your points e.g. *'Schama claims that the Normans changed "loyalty" in England and this is true as William introduced the Feudal System which...'*
Paragraphs The best answers contain paragraphs which always focus on the question and link back to the question at the end of each.					Go back through your paragraphs rewrite any final sentences that do not link back to the question, e.g. *'Therefore, _____ proves that the Normans did bring considerable trouble to England'*
Structure The best answers will have a clear structure, with each paragraph having a clear theme and a separate conclusion.					Rewrite any paragraph that has muddled to themes together, such as giving examples of both agreeing and disagreeing, e.g. it has talked about improvements for women and also the rebellions.
SPaG The best answers will have a accurate spelling of keywords use capital letters and uses a wide range of vocabulary.					Rewrite your spelling corrections in the margin three times and rewrite any sentences that need correcting which the teacher has highlighted. Common mistakes include Feudal System, Thegn and Earl.
Teacher feedback					

Whole Class Feedback

1. Make any improvements/changes to your own answer in red pen.
2. Tick anything you did well on.
3. Complete the two tasks your teacher has given you.

....
....
....
....
....
....
....
....
....
....
....
....

My department can go through student assessments or classwork in 10-30 minutes and complete a WCF sheet, which they turn into valuable feedback lessons that focuses on re-teaching content through direct instruction, remodelling and practising disciplinary skills, redrafting or simply reiterating expectations over presentation and effort. Throughout these 'feedback' lessons (we've renamed 'DIRT'), students also receive personal verbal feedback as this is noted down by the teacher and time is taken to discuss with them during the feedback lesson. WCF has also become a valuable tool to highlight the clear and high expectations of the teacher and school.

On the workload front, it has 'saved' many of those who teach eight-plus different classes and we feel, as a department, we are more responsive than ever. We use both informal discussions and department time to share and discuss our WCF findings, which allowed us to preempt issues with our own classes and helped any curriculum changes for the future.

Over time, our feedback policy has continued to evolve and we have moved to WCF for assessment marking also. As we mark assessments we grade a student's assessment from 1-4 using task-specific feedback in three areas (knowledge, skills and communication) and then highlight two follow-up tasks based on the areas students have struggled on. To accompany this, a sheet is also completed which allows teachers to provide task-specific feedback to the assessment, this is shared with the students during the following feedback lesson. Both staff and teacher voice is particularly positive towards these methods of feedback and, as a school, our results have continued to improve these last four years. This could be causation or correlation, but WCF has certainly had a big impact on our department and students.

Norman conquest assessment feedback

Highlight your WWW/EBI Codes your teacher has written

WWW Codes	EBI Codes
LY – Excellent written communication and sentence structure	**LY** – Think about the language you use and how you structure your sentences
Q – You've used a number of quotes from Schama to support your point	**Q** – Make sure you use a quote from the interpretation in your answer
EX – Great examples used to support your answers	**EX** – Include more examples to explain your points
A/D – You've written a balanced agree/disagree answer	**A/D** – You must write both agree and disagree paragraphs
CN – Conclusion clearly summarised your opinion on Schama's view	**CN** – Your conclusion needs summarise your overall opinion using key point to support it
SK – Brilliant specific knowledge used throughout	**SK** – I want more specific dates, figures and facts in your answer
L – Each paragraph links back to the question, explaining 'why' you agree or disagree	**L** – Make sure each paragraph links back to the question, to explain your point
	STQ – Please stick to the question
	D – You answer lacks detail and effort

Easy Feedback

Knowledge Fixes: Bits we, as a class, struggled on

Assessment Stars
Brilliant performances from:

SPaG Feedback
Mainly capital letter issues:

Do Now Tasks:

I have recently created a document on using whole class feedback and its application in the history classroom for 'History How To's', a collaborative project I've set up between history practitioners. It encompasses the journey I have made with whole class feedback during these last four years.

History
How To's

Whole Class Feedback

Greg Thornton
@mrthorntonteach

What is Whole Class Feedback
WCF is a formative feedback approach where a teacher looks over student work and identifies

What does the research say?
There is no specific research into WCF, but we do have a wealth of research on the power of feedback

The key findings of the 2016 EEF report found that *'There is little high quality research.... to suggest that extensive or detailed marking has any significant impact on learning'*

Many have argued we need to shift to 'Less marking, more feedback', with Christodoulou highlighting the impact of traditional marking on workload.

William has argued feedback must instead *"improve the pupil, not just the work".* To really make feedback work, it *"must provide a recipe for future action"* To support this, Fletcher Wood has identified what we must do with feedback to be beneficial; *Reteach, Revisit, Redraft*

Further Reading
Responsive Teaching: Fletcher Wood;
Howard: Stop Talking About Wellbeing

Reteach → Revisit goals → Revise process → Redraft Practice Check

Using Whole Class Feedback
This guide tells you how to complete whole class feedback,

Praise & EBI
These are valuable boxes to highlight student work/effort in the classroom or as a push for students to improve. Evidence of success from those in the class can offer motivation.

Presentation
Use this in Term 1 to push and model expectations on book presentation.

Polaroid Moments
Spotlight excellent in the classroom. These can be student answers or work to be used as models in feedback.

History Marking Crib Sheet Date: Class:

Praise	Feedback	Literacy Key Terms
		SPaG
Even Better If		Activities
Presentation	Polaroid Moments	

Feedback
This is where issues and misconceptions are logged. This informs what your will be focus in the feedback lesson
This section can influence how you teach a lesson/skill next time.

Literacy
Highlight any errors on SPaG

Activities
These are next step tasks, they should be precise and actionable, giving students an opportunity to improve their work, consolidate knowledge or practice. Number these for each student.

Using WCF
Here is guidance on how you use WCF

1 Choose a task, assessment or lessons work to look over

2 Read through the books and complete a Whole Class Feedback sheet

3 Decide what to focus on in your feedback lesson

4 Provide WCF to reteach content, revisit skill/models to improve students

5 Give students time to practice, redraft and apply knowledge to task or their existing work

6 Monitor issues over amend curriculum

In the History Classroom
Below are some examples of how you could use Whole Class Feedback and what you could do next

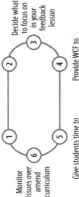

Examiners Report
Create a class report based on a mock exam. Use model answers, give WWW/EBI for the class and reteach.

Live Marking
Pick a model from WCF and 'live mark' under the visualizer and get students mark own.

Sampling
Short on time? Pick just 4/5 books from a class and do a spot WCF sheet on those.

Comparison
Pull two essays (weak & strong) for the class to compare and note the difference. Then compare to own answer.

75

Guided feedback

We know from our discussions so far that the role of feedback can be powerful in supporting pupils to move forward in their learning. Alongside the use of whole class feedback, we can combine this with guided feedback to support pupils in their next steps. If we want pupils to accept our feedback, we need them to feel that the next steps are within their reach. This is where guiding them along their improvement journey is crucial to get build the receptive culture, which we talked about in chapter 1. The following template provides an example of how you can guide pupils through your feedback to enable them to feedforward into subsequent tasks that require them to apply the same skill.

Success criteria	1. Misconceptions		
Level 1 (Basic) (1-3 marks) A basic answer. Simple description of the role of tourism in reducing the development gap. The answer is generic with limited assessment of the validity of the statement. Frequent SPaG errors.	M1: The reduction in tourist numbers in the winter may not necessarily result in everyone going bankrupt.		
	2. Improvements		
	I1: Introduction – location of Tunisia at the beginning I2: Split points into separate paragraphs I3: Use PDL structure I4: Ensure two to three developed paragraphs I5: Use data/evidence in your answer I6: Ensure points are linked to how tourism contributes towards addressing the development gap I7: Provide a substantiated conclusion that answers the validity of the view I8: Proofread your response to check for SPAG errors		
Level 2 (Clear) (4-6 marks) A clear answer, with at least two specific explanations of the role of tourism in reducing the development gap. The answer may contain some examples to support the points made and partial judgement. Few SPaG errors.			
Level 3 (Detailed) (7-9 marks) An explicit answer, with **a range** of specific explanations on the role of tourism with examples to support the points made and a thorough judgement of the validity. Limited SPaG errors.	**3. SPaG** Libya Algeria Desert Pollution Therefore Neighbourhood Northern Decrease	**4. Praise** Structure: Data: Explanations:	**5. Check your book** THUD (title, hypothesis, underlined, date) Highlight VIFs and hypothesis responses, glue in any sheets

Guided feedback

Read the following response and reflect on the following questions.

1. Where is there evidence that this response is talking about Tunisia?
2. Does this response refer to the impact on the development gap?
3. What could be added to improve the assessment of the statement from the question set?

> The growth of tourism can reduce the development gap by thousands of tourists visiting it per year causing them to bring in a lot of income for the country to develop. The evidence shows that tourists were bringing in $3 billion per year. This can help the country to develop by then being able to afford better health care and for them to improve their houses etc.

Teacher Spotlight: Balancing the complexities of feedback

NEIL ALMOND, ASSISTANT HEADTEACHER IN PRIMARY EDUCATION

Neil Almond is an assistant headteacher for teaching and learning across a small, four-school trust in the primary sector around the south-east London/Kent border. He is passionate about making sure that students receive the best education possible by implementing the 'best bets' that educational research and cognitive science signpost so that everyone gets the best possible chance when they leave primary school to flourish at secondary school and beyond. His role has seen lead on develop curricula for all four schools and working with teachers to implement research-informed techniques in the classroom.

He blogs on other areas of education at nutsaboutteaching.wordpress.com and you can find him tweeting as @Mr_AlmondED

When thinking about effective feedback, it is important to consider and carefully balance student achievement, student motivation and teacher workload. For too long at the primary level, there was the expectation of all work to be marked in-depth before the next lesson. That means that for the average class of 30 students, primary teachers would be expected to mark around 90 pieces of work (30 English,

30 reading and 30 maths) within 24 hours and ensure that lessons that would take place in the afternoon were all marked for. Not only is this unsustainable but it offered very little gains when compared to the time put it in. Now, a growing trend of using verbal feedback in the classroom is growing and while on the surface the act of providing students with feedback may seem quite straightforward, the research on this topic can often be confusing and contradictory.

At Woodland Academy Trust (WAT) we are clear that by feedback, we mean that the teachers' efforts into providing feedback are not for the improvement of a piece of work, but rather to improve the student. After synthesising available evidence into feedback, we created an evidence-informed marking policy that heavily uses whole class feedback (WCF) where appropriate. This was trialled by a working party to ensure that the policy was fit for purpose before rolling it out in the 2020-21 academic year. The following gives an example of what this policy will look like in the classroom.

Teachers will deliver three types of feedback to the class: shout out, rapid recap and challenge, though students will not have to respond to all three. The shout out will identify students who have successfully gone above and beyond in meeting the learning objective from the previous lesson or have done anything that the teacher feels is worthy of a shout out. For example, solving a problem in maths using an original method or writing a complex, grammatically correct sentence with excellent use of language in English. Where possible, the work will be shared with the class along with an explanation of why the work has been deemed worthy of a shout out. All students must attend to this.

The rapid recap allows for targeted questions based on common misconceptions, common errors or elements of the success criteria for the previous lesson that the students did not meet. What this looks like will depend on the subject. It could be a quick recap of some chronological events in history, a chance for the students to relabel a diagram in geography or search for specific errors related to last lessons learning in a piece of writing before identifying it in their writing from the previous day. How a teacher identifies students who need to partake in the rapid recap is left to their discretion.

The challenge part of the WCF allows those students who have successfully met the objective from the previous lesson the opportunity to extend their thinking. This is not the case where each child will be tasked with a different challenge, but from looking at the students work, the teacher can identify an appropriate challenge that will meet the needs of the students who require this challenge. For example, if over two lessons students have learnt about rivers and canals, an appropriate challenge might be to get students to then compare these two geographic features. In maths this could include being able to represent a mathematical idea in as many representations as possible, or for English it could be to rewrite a passage in a different tense or from the perspective of another character. Again, how the teacher signals which student do the challenge aspect is up to their discretion.

Feedback from the working party has been positive in that it has helped cut the amount of time teachers spend traditionally marking books while increasing students' level of engagement with feedback when compared to the old solution of written marking. We look forward to rolling this policy across all schools so that all teachers and students can benefit from it. Leaders within the schools will monitor its impact across the academic year where we hope that all members of the school communities will see an improvement in the quality of learning that takes place.

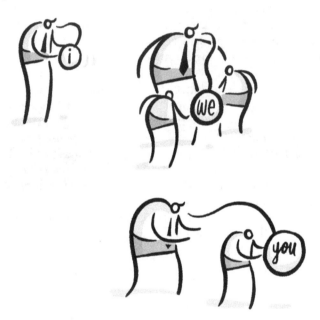

2.4 I, We, You

Here is one I made earlier! The process of modelling is a vital component in any classroom and a key cog to contributing towards learning. The use of teacher modelling in the classroom can help to dispel misconceptions before they begin. If we can model excellence and participate the misconceptions pupils frequently have about a particular concept or process in our subjects this can help to reduce the amount of feedback we need to give to pupils later on in the learning journey. The 'I, We, You' approach to modelling provides an opportunity to create lessons that guide practice and release the scaffolded support when pupils have a chance to practice independently.

Live modelling is a powerful way to provide front-loaded feedback to pupils as you take them through the process of constructing an answer. This allows pupils to watch you, as the expert, to guide them through the steps required to construct a response that would meet the intended success criteria. Of course, this requires a degree of confidence and it is always useful to practise your modelling of explanations, something I delve further into in chapter 4.

Once you have walked pupils through the process of constructing a response that would meet the success criteria it is then important to allow time for pupils to practice themselves. If the task pupils complete is too similar to the modelled example it could mean that pupils will merely copy the teacher model without actually attempting to apply the knowledge they have learnt themselves. To avoid this, it is always useful to model something similar but to then provide the opportunity for pupils to independently practice in a different context. For example, if I was teaching pupils how to apply their understanding of landform formation, I might model how to do this with cliffs and wave-cut platforms. Then, as a class, we would co-construct a response on the formation of headlands and bays, and finally, in the 'you' part, pupils would independently construct a response for the formation of cave, arches, stacks and stumps. In demonstrating the process involved in writing about the formation of landform at the beginning through modelling, pupils then have sufficient knowledge to practise this process themselves but in the context of a different landform. This alleviates the possibility of pupils merely copying my model. An example and copy of the worksheet follow.

River and coastal landscapes: Describe and explain question practice

1. Describe and explain the formation of a coastal bar. (6 marks)

2. Describe and explain the impacts of coastal erosion on this landscape. (6 Marks)

Step 1: 'I' Worked Example
Read through my example I have written, then highlight the 3 key sections

The formation of the bar in Figure 1 will begin with the south-westerly prevailing wind causing the waves swash to push sediment up the beach at an angle. The backwash will result in a zig zag movement of material along the coastline, known as longshore drift. As shown in Figure 1 the direction of longshore drift is transporting sediment from west to east.

When there is a change in the direction of the coastline, usually because of an estuary or a bay, the transported material is deposited offshore as the waves lose energy. Overtime the build-up of material off the coast will cause a spit to form, stretching across from the headland in an easterly direction. The spit will continue to grow until it eventually connects to a headland on the other side. Fresh or slightly salty water is trapped behind the bar, causing a lagoon to form.

☐ Sequence   ☐ Processess   ☐ Figure

Step 2: 'We' Joint Construction
Lets collaboratively write an answer for the waterfall figure on the board

The formation of the waterfall in Figure 2b begins when..

Step 3: 'We' Completion Model 2
With the teacher and your neighbour, complete the sentences, remember to use PDL

The coastal landscape illustrated by the two images in Figure 2b, indicates the coastline has experiences erosion because...

Secondly, the images demonstrate buildings have disappeared over the 16 years, which will have impacted the local area because..

Step 4: 'You' Independent Example
Independently write an answer to the question on the board: Remember SPF

☐ Sequence   ☐ Processess   ☐ Figure

There might be occasions when you want to share a model that illustrates deliberate errors. This might be done through live modelling or one that you have constructed prior to the lesson. These deliberate errors can demonstrate what pupils should avoid doing and help them to prepare to not repeat this in their own work. There are times when I will deliberately make a mistake live and pupils will instinctively correct me.

Modelling is a powerful way to provide pupils with front-loaded feedback prior to them independently practising. Rosenshine (2012) indicated that the most effective teachers provide models because providing students with models and worked examples can help them learn to solve problems faster. Rosenshine highlighted from his research that when teachers provide models and articulate their thinking during the construction of the model this provides effective cognitive support.

2.5 Peer and self-feedback

The role of peer assessment in contributing towards learning has been debated in recent years. In the past, my experience of peer feedback has been pupils providing marks and comments on one of their peer's work. All too often this ended up with these generic unhelpful comments that didn't allow for meaningful improvement.

'Well done, you have done everything you needed to do for this piece of work.'

'Great work.'

'I don't think you need to make any improvements.'

Alongside these generic comments, pupils can have negative thoughts about the role of peer assessment in supporting their learning.

'It's not my job to mark work.'

'I'm not the expert, the teacher is. I don't know how many marks to award this piece of work.'

'I don't agree with these marks, Miss.'

As we discussed in the opening chapter there are the three feedback triggers of truth, identity and relationship to consider here. When I have asked pupils in the past to give feedback on one of their peer's work this can lead to two scenarios unfolding. The first one is the person giving the feedback is one of their friends and provides positive feedback on their work because they have a positive relationship. Happy days. Consequently, the person accepts the generic feedback as being the truth. However, if the person providing the feedback is not one of their close friends this leads to all sorts of problems. Frequently, when the pupil receives the feedback they tend to disagree with it and ask for my second opinion. The perception of the credibility of the person providing them with the feedback is questioned because ultimately they don't see their peer as an expert. This was highlighted by Li, Liu and Steckelberg (2009): 'While students express their appreciation of the opportunity to actively participate in the assessment and learning process, they also state concern regarding the quality and quantity of peer assessment received.'

So, does this mean we shouldn't use peer assessment in lessons? For me, the problem here is the belief that we should provide opportunities for pupils to assess the work of their peers. The connotations of the word 'assessment' over 'feedback' when introducing peer work with pupils is significant because assessment suggests that it is high stakes and there will be marks awarded. However, what we can ask them to do is provide 'guided peer feedback'.

The value of peer feedback is recognised in supporting and enhancing learning. When pupils have the opportunity to read their peers work this allows them to see examples and identify graduations in quality (Sadler, 1989) and therefore generate a greater awareness of the strengths and flaws in their own. The more we create opportunities for pupils to read their peers work, the more we equip pupils with having a greater awareness of the solutions required for their own pieces of work, developing a deeper conceptual understanding. When pupils return to their work they can decide if they have sufficiently met the success criteria. So, if peer feedback can provide a positive contribution towards learning what can we do to support this in lessons?

To combine the use of peer and self-assessment the cycle illustrated on the following page provides a framework to connect them, which is centred around four phases: task performance, feedback provision, feedback reception and revision.

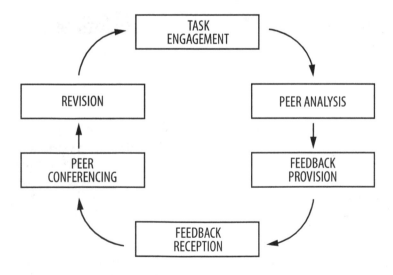

Here are a few suggestions that you could adopt when building in peer feedback opportunities in your own lessons.

1. **Create the 'buy in'** – share the reason why peer feedback is part of the learning process with your pupils and clarify that it isn't about awarding each other marks or grades.
2. **Initial peer conversations** – allow pupils to talk about the application task they will be doing before beginning to work. Encourage pupils to have an open conversation by considering the following questions before they begin the task: *'What are you planning on doing?' 'Why have you decided to take that approach?'*
3. **Explicit success criteria** – provide pupils with success criteria that they understand and can explicitly identify in the work. For example, when pupils are exploring the physical processes that cause the formation of distinctive coastal landforms one of the success criteria is to include physical processes such as hydraulic action. This is clearer than expecting pupils to identify if one of their pieces has provided a detailed explanation.
4. **Practice** – create plenty of opportunities for pupils to practise providing feedback to their peers to increase their confidence.

In the following spotlights, David Goodwin shares how he has structured booklets to provide feedback to his pupils and Jade Pearce provides an insight into how her school have launched a no written feedback policy.

Teacher Spotlight: The role of booklets and feedback

DAVID GOODWIN, TEACHER AND HEAD OF YEAR

David is a geography teacher and the head of Years 10 and 11 at a school in north-east Lincolnshire. He has held a variety of positions in his teaching career including head of faculty, SLE and pupil premium coordinator. David is currently co-writing a book with Oliver Caviglioli called *Organise Ideas: Graphic Organisers for Meaningful Learning*, due to be published in 2021. You can find him tweeting as @MrGoodwin23

Imagine, if you will, a recently qualified teacher. Today, they have a full timetable to teach and spend their lunch break photocopying worksheets for the afternoon. Despite getting to school early they still lose their lunchtime. Now imagine me. It is Wednesday, I teach five (out of five) lessons and lead an assembly. I spend my lunch break rehearsing my explanation for the difficult topic I am going to teach this afternoon. I make a note of the pupils I suspect will need additional scaffolding and also who I will target during cold call questioning. In this hectic teaching day, I need to keep my focus and what works for me is a homemade booklet.

Well-designed booklets are like custom textbooks created by Barak Rosenshine. The one I am using on Wednesday afternoon took a long time to create. But now I am reaping the benefits. While there are no easy ways to write a booklet, Rosenshine's 'Principles of Instruction' gives you plenty of simple and practical ideas. For the teacher, booklets are time-saving and offer constant memory prompts that free up their working memory. For the pupil, they are almost a virtual teacher providing information in a meaningful sequence, opportunities for independent work and self-checking and are always available which is especially crucial if they ever miss a lesson.

The lesson begins with me handing pupils their booklets as they enter. No worksheets, no glue sticks or scissors — just one resource, maximising learning time. Today, pupils will be learning about the Indian monsoon. We begin with retrieval practice. Ordinarily, this is composed of low stakes recall — five questions with links to prior and today's intended learning. Plus, five questions to allow for spaced practice. Today's lesson is no different. Tom Sherrington shares a wonderful analogy about a climbing wall instructor I'd like to explain. The instructor doesn't just check the harness of one climber and assume all the other are safe. She checks them all. With this firmly in mind, I scan the room, I walk around the classroom, I look over pupils' shoulders, I read their work – all in the attempt to find out what they don't understand. Once finished, pupils self-assess their responses and immediately receive their first piece of feedback. No pupils are missed.

To ensure pupils understand the content they have practised retrieving – and not merely recalled it – we will follow up with cold call questioning. 'Right class, we are going to cold call this question: why are equatorial regions the warmest in the world?' My class knows this means no hands up, think hard and be prepared to share your thinking. After 30 seconds of silent thinking time, I ask 'Mary, what do you think?' Notice the language I use? It is inviting. At this stage, I want feedback about what they don't know more than what they do know. Having the confidence to share errors, doubts or misconceptions is key to their learning. This sort of feedback tells me if I need to re-teach and, like our climbing wall instructor, if it is safe to move on. I've now checked for understanding and can confidently begin teaching new content. A hallmark of a great booklet is pupils reading for meaning. Notice the subtle, faded numbers preceding each line of text? 'James please can you read lines 1 to 5, and Chloe would you kindly read lines 6 to 10?' While reading, I stop the class and ask 'Marvin, in lines 5 and 6, it refers to India as a subcontinent. What is your understanding of this term?' This 'in the moment feedback' is king. Much like the coach of a golfer correcting their clients' swing, we can swiftly correct errors or misconceptions. That way, pupils won't put errors into their long-term memory. It is feedback in the moment.

Careful reading of the booklet by the pupils can lead to better and more extended writing. Ruth Walker has written a glorious blog in which she proposes a model I have found to be effective for achieving this. The model is sequenced as follows. After pupils read a piece of text, they answer comprehension questions about it. Pupils then transform the text into an appropriate graphic organiser, they practise writing sophisticated sentences – using activities from the Writing Revolution – and finally, complete extended writing tasks. This class is experienced in creating graphic organisers, but I know some still require scaffolding. I distribute partially completed organisers and worked examples of similar but different content. With the knowledge organised and transformed into a non-linear spatial array, the class can begin practising how they will communicate their understanding. They do this by first practising the use of appositives to create sophisticated sentences and follow it up with an extended piece of writing.

Tonight I will read through all my pupils work, especially the extended pieces of writing. I will make notes of all the strengths and a list of errors, misconceptions, spelling mistakes and any other areas for improvement. This feedback will be shared next lesson and because it is shared publically I refrain from attaching errors to individuals. In the next lesson, I will use the visualiser to showcase examples of excellent work (alternatively take a photo) and areas in need of improvement. The focus of this whole class feedback is to move learning forward. I refrain from vague comments such as 'improve your introductions' and opt for specific feedback, such as: 'In your introductions, use an appositive to tell me what the word monsoon means.' In some cases – if as a class there are common errors and misconceptions – I might be required to re-teach some of the content. To ensure knowledge gaps have been addressed I will use similar but different questions to those from the previous lesson. I do this to check the knowledge if flexible, meaning pupils' can use it to answer different questions. This helps improve the learner and not just the most recent piece of work. Moves learning forward by improving future performance.

While everything I have described could be achieved without the creation of a booklet, they allow me to outsource my thinking, freeing up my working memory to give timely and effective feedback. The careful thinking behind their creation means I can focus on teaching and feedback. And, for the pupil, they have a valuable resource for revision. I will summarise my thoughts about feedback with this simple maxim: All pupils. In the moment. Moves learning forward.

Differential heating and India's unique geography drives the monsoon

In our last sequence of learning, we learnt about India's unique location as a subcontinent and how this affects their levels of social and economic development. In this next sequence, we shall study:

- How India's monsoon occurs
- The importance of the monsoon for economic and social development

What is a monsoon

The word 'monsoon' comes from the Arabic word mausim, meaning "season". The seasonal wind change brings with it intense levels of precipitation and it is caused by the unique location and geography of the Indian subcontinent. To understand its causes, we need to first understand why do we have different seasons.

2. What does the term subcontinent mean?

_____

_____

_____

A monsoon is a seasonal change in wind patterns

Monsoon

↓

Comes from the Arabic word mausim, meaning seasons

↓

British sailors first sailed to India in the 1600s

↓

British sailors translated mausim to **monsoon** and used this word to describe the winds blowing across the Arabian Sea and Bay of Bengal

It takes Earth 365 days to complete full a orbit of the sun

Why do we have seasons?

Seasons are caused by the earth orbiting the sun. It takes the Earth 365 days to complete a full orbit. While orbiting the Sun the Earth is also rotating on its axis. It takes the earth 24 hours, one full day to rotate 360 degrees on its axis. This is why we have night and day, areas of the Earth facing the Sun, experience daylight, whilst those not facing the Sun will experience night time.

The Earth takes 24 hours to rotate 360 degrees on its axis

Teacher Spotlight: The launch of no written marking

JADE PEARCE, TEACHER AND ASSISTANT HEADTEACHER

Jade is a business studies/economics teacher and assistant headteacher at a high school in Staffordshire. She has been teaching for 12 years and has held many roles including head of department, head of house, SLE and subject expert for an initial teacher training provider. She is an evidence lead in education for Staffordshire Research School. She has completed her MA in Education and is currently completing her NPQH. She is passionate about evidence-informed pedagogy, curriculum, reducing workload and CPD. She can be found tweeting as @PearceMrs

Our journey towards no requirement for written marking has been a long one. Previously, teachers have been expected to regularly write comments or questions on pupils work which pupils then had to respond to. Their response had to viewed and often commented on again. Quality assurance was also heavily focused on book scrutiny and the extent to which pupils' work had been marked. This was a method of marking that I, as a teacher and later a leader, was also fully committed to. I was proud of my marking and believed that only by writing comments which told pupils exactly how to improve their work could they make progress.

Over time, this certainty in the power of written marking started to fade. The criticisms that have already been explained many times (the time taken, the opportunity cost of this time, workload issues, the lack of independence developed by pupils and the pupils making the same mistakes in late work) started to become evident over time. As a result of this I started to look at alternatives to writing long comments on pupils' work. There are numerous examples of studies, research papers and blogs which explained these alternatives, and this gave me a starting point. I formed a teaching and learning group of teachers who were interested in alternatives to written marking. Together, we read and discussed the techniques and each member chose one or two techniques that they wanted to trial. We met numerous times throughout the year to evaluate the implementation and refine the new approaches we were using.

I then presented these alternative approaches (namely modelling, live feedback, using a visualiser, self-assessment and whole class verbal feedback) to the rest of the teaching staff. This was done through a whole school teaching and learning briefing. I explained the benefits of reducing written marking and described and modelled how each of the techniques could be used. The staff guide to 'No Written Marking' was given as a supporting handout for staff to refer back to. I followed this up with a step-by-step guide so that staff could see how these methods could be used 'in-action'.

Following this, whole-school introduction departments were given time to discuss, decide and plan how these alternatives could best be implemented in their subject and lessons. This was in no way prescribed with different departments taking different approaches. This helped to give ownership to teachers and gained initial buy-in. During this time, any members of the teaching and learning group acted as both champions of the approach and relative 'experts' to give more guidance to other members of their department. It was also crucial to gain buy-in from pupils, parents and governors. We communicated the proposed changes, the reasons for them and the supporting research to each of these groups. We reassured them that we would continue to consult with them throughout the year.

When these techniques were starting to be implemented across the school we gave as much support as possible including coaching, sharing of best practice from within the school, and giving constructive feedback from any lesson drop-ins. We ensured that this initiative kept the momentum and started to be embedded across the school over the year by regularly giving time for teachers to reflect on, evaluate and improve upon their practice.

Key takeaways

- Providing feedback is a challenge and one that needs to be sustainable for teachers and pupils.
- For feedback to provide a meaningful contribution to the learning process what we teach and how we teach it needs to be well thought out.
- Allow sufficient time to return and check on progress to reinforces to the pupil your commitment to the feedback process.
- The significance of how good a question is determined by its effectiveness as a tool to invoke the right emotions and thoughts.
- Planning the questions is only the first step, we need to ensure we create the conditions where our pupils want to respond.
- Deliberate errors can demonstrate what pupils should avoid doing and help them to prepare to not repeat this in their own work.
- Create opportunities for pupils to read their peers work, which will generate greater awareness of the solutions required for their own pieces of work.

QR codes for chapter resources

Chapter reflections

Use the space below to reflect on how you plan to provide feedback to your pupils.

Chapter 2 references

Alexander, R. J. (2017) *Towards Dialogic Teaching: rethinking classroom talk* (5th ed). Cambridge: Dialogos.

Balibar, F. (ed.) (2002) *Physique, philosophie, politique.* Paris: Éditions du Seuil.

Brualdi Timmins, A. C. (1998) 'Classroom Questions', *Practical Assessment, Research, and Evaluation* 6 (6).

Ellis, R., Loewen, S. and Erlam, R. (2006) 'Implicit and explicit corrective feedback and the acquisition of grammar', *Studies in Second Language Acquisition* 28 (2) pp. 339-368.

Filippone, M. (1998) 'Questioning at the Elementary Level' [Dissertation]. Retrieved from: www.bit.ly/37jzLxl

Li, L., Liu, X. and Steckelburg, A. L. (2009) 'Assessor or assessee: How student learning improves by giving and receiving peer feedback', *British Journal of Educational Technology* 41 (3) pp. 525-536.

Myatt, M. (2018) *The Curriculum: Gallimaufry to Coherence.* Woodbridge: John Catt Educational.

Pate, R. T. and Bremer, N. H. (1967) 'Guiding Learning Through Skilful Questioning', *The Elementary School Journal* 67 (8) pp. 417-422.

Rosenshine, B. (2012) 'Principles of Instruction', *American Educator.* Retrieved from: www.bit.ly/3lD447Q

Sadler, D. R. (1989) 'Formative assessment and the design of instructional systems', *Instructional Science* 18 pp. 119-144.

University City London (2019) 'UCL Verbal Feedback Project Report 2019'. Retrieved from: www.bit.ly/2HccfJC

Wilen, W. W. and Clegg, A. A. (1986) 'Effective questions and questioning: A research review', *Theory and Research in Social Education* 14 (2) pp. 153-161.

Wragg E. C. (1993) *Questioning in the Primary Classroom.* London: Routledge.

3

FEEDBACK TO TEACHERS: CHANGING THE HISTORICAL CPD CULTURE

'If we want teachers to get better at something as complex as teaching, we need to provide the same conditions we provide for our students to support their learning.'
– Professor Rob Coe

Chapter checklist

✓ Teaching is complex, and we should provide teachers with the time to develop their practice

✓ Teacher education should be given dedicated time to allow for deliberate practice

✓ Teacher observations should be about empowering others to improve their practice

✓ Feedback should guide teachers to practising one skill at a time

✓ Provide teachers with models to support practising the skill they are aiming to develop

✓ Create a culture where teachers have the time and space to practise and master a skill

✓ Teacher education should support the development of teachers into responsive practitioners

3.1 The problem with teacher education

A scenario...

Tom, an English teacher in his third year of teaching, is waiting for feedback from his latest formal observation. Prior to the lesson observation, Tom was told he was being observed and prepared his lesson to ensure he impressed the observer. The pressure of this one-off yearly observation linked to his performance management always feels high stakes. He knows he needs to 'perform' and impress. After the lesson, he receives his feedback. The observer provides him with guidance on how he performed and what he needs to do to improve. He gets three targets including, 'develop your use of questioning'. Tom signs the paperwork for the year and struggles to understand how he can improve his use of questioning. His observer suggests he goes and visits Sarah who is excellent at questioning.

The goal...

Harry, a science teacher in his second year of teaching, knows he will be receiving feedback at the end of the day. The observer sent a quick email to Harry as per his request to enable him to have an opportunity to prepare for the coaching conversation. This helps to reduce Harry's stress and the observer was conscious to make sure he asked him how he wanted to receive his feedback. The feedback provides Harry with a clear action step to work on to improve his practice over the coming weeks the observer works with him to model how he could implement this in his lesson. Harry is left feeling this next step is achievable.

The professional development of staff is a vital element to developing a positive culture of learning in schools. We want teachers to feel supported, empowered and develop into consciously competent practitioners that continually reflect on how they can support every pupil and their colleagues to succeed.

To quote Shaun Allison and Andy Tharby, we should aim to make 'every lesson count'. No matter what stage of your career you are currently at, every teacher wants every lesson to be the best for each and every one of their pupils. I am sure that as a teacher you have experienced that magical moment where one of your pupils or your class just get it. That feeling is magical and one of the best feelings because this is the reason why we decided to teach – to make a difference and inspire the younger generation.

Getting teacher education right in schools is important to the morale and wellbeing of teachers. The more teachers feel their own professional development is valued, the greater the motivation to get better. We find ourselves in a decade where teacher recruitment and retention is at an all-time low. So much so that in 2019 the Department for Education launched a teacher recruitment and retention strategy. Damien Hinds, the then Education Secretary, introduced this strategy by commenting: 'I wanted us to take an unflinching look at the problems, and to listen to what teachers and headteachers had to say about how to begin to solve them. Developed collaboratively with the profession and experts across the sector, this document sets out the government's priorities for making sure a career in teaching continues to be attractive, sustainable and rewarding.'

Alongside this vision to support the future of our profession the DfE outlined for a world-class education system to flourish:

1. Get the balance right between holding schools to account and helping them to improve.
2. Make the job manageable again, eradicating unnecessary workload and developing arrangements that support flexible working.
3. Invest in and embed school cultures that create a sense of value through ongoing professional development. (Department for Education, 2019)

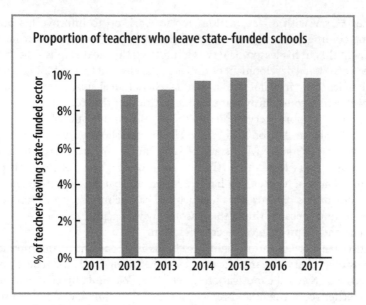

Department for Education (2018)

For many years teachers have found themselves in the same situation as Tom, frustrated by the constant spotlight to prove they are doing a good job instead of a drive to support professional development that focuses on supporting teacher improvement. It is one of the main reasons why teachers leave the profession and the Department for Education (2019) indicated that 'over 20% of new teachers leave the profession within their first two years of teaching, and 33% leave within their first five years'.

Alongside the challenges of the recruitment and retention of teachers in the profession is the retention of teachers in schools that serve disadvantaged communities. In these schools, one in ten teachers chooses to leave for another secondary school, as well as struggling to recruit specialist teachers for specific subjects (Department for Education, 2016; Sibieta, 2018). In 2017/18, the 'Get Into Teaching' website indicated 150,000 people registered to show an interest in teaching but only 45,000 actually applied for mainstream postgraduate teacher training (UCAS, 2018).

In many of these more challenging schools, the workload is unmanageable and there is an unhealthy focus on the core accountability measure of key headline figures based on the outcomes in English and maths. This tunnelled vision leads to the continual change of systems as leaders try to implement the next 'buzz' strategy to bring about improvement. Inevitably, for the classroom teacher, these strategies are not given the time to embed or review, leaving many frustrated practitioners and ultimately low staff morale.

This merry-go-round of continual implementation of strategies leads to a top-down approach to teacher education where CPD is ticked off through delivering sessions on the lastest research-based evidence but with little focus on how to effectively support teachers in implementing them over time in the classroom to improve teacher practice. Inevitably, teachers end up on a cycle of teaching, marking, submitting data based on their pupil performance and then leaders observing and making judgements on their effectiveness. This feedback to teachers is often lacking the depth and clarity to provide meaningful feedback. This leads to what Hogarth (2001) referred to as wicked learning environments.

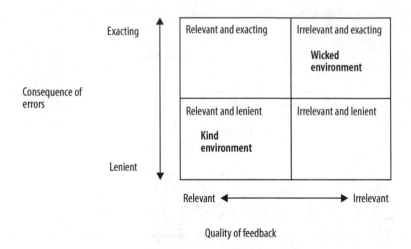

Hogarth's learning structure from *Educating Intuition* (2001)

Hogarth's learning structure (2001) indicated that when feedback was relevant learning will be accurate and not create false beliefs. When 'wicked' environments exist, this creates irrelevant and confusing feedback. He provided the following example from a medical perspective to illustrate his point: 'The physician enjoyed the reputation of a diagnostician, with a particular skill in diagnosing typhoid fever, then the commonest disease on the wards of New York's hospitals. He placed particular reliance on the appearance of the tongue, which was universal in the medicine of the day (now entirely inexplicable, long forgotten). He believed he could detect significant differences by palpating that organ. The ward rounds conducted by this man were, essentially, tongue rounds; each patient would stick out his tongue while the eminence took it between thumb and forefinger, feeling its textures and irregularities, then moving from bed to bed, diagnosing typhoid fever in its earliest stages over and over again, and turning out a week or so later to have been right, to everyone's amazement. He was a more effective carrier, using only his hands, than Typhoid Mary.'

In this example, the feedback that the doctor received was in a wicked environment, it was irrelevant and enacting. You cannot learn in a wicked environment (Hogarth, 2001). However, when feedback is accurate, creating kind environments, it provides the opportunity to create the conditions in which learning can thrive. In schools where teachers receive quality feedback that provides concrete targets through instructional coaching, this has the potential to create collaborative and supportive environments to enable teachers to develop and improve their practice. This is supported by the findings from Kini and Podolsky's (2016) review on teacher effectiveness: 'Teachers' effectiveness increases at a greater rate when they teach in a supportive and collegial working environment, and when they accumulate experience in the same grade level, subject or district.'

Every school has the potential to create systems that put teacher education at the heart of everything they do. After all, teacher education is not just important for the professional development of staff it is vital in supporting teachers to be equipped with the knowledge on how they can best approach teaching their pupils. Therefore, establishing systems that create quality teacher education is crucial to future recruitment and retention.

3.2 Teacher professional development

Teacher professional development in schools is commonly referred to as 'continuous professional development (CPD)' with many schools providing this through external speakers invited to present on research-based approaches, twilight sessions and dedicated time allocated for department leads to disseminate whole-school approaches. More recently to coincide with the greater use of research to inform practice, schools have invested in research lead roles.

In the 'Great Teaching Toolkit' (2020) by Evidence Based Education, Dr Tristian Stobie outlines the importance of teacher development: 'Teaching should be a rewarding profession where teachers are empowered and supported to be the best creative professionals they can be. The overwhelming body of research finds that the most important factor in improving student outcomes is good teaching. Therefore, helping teachers become better is the most important responsibility we have as educational leaders, as it is the best way to help learners fulfil their potential.'

In my personal experience, the CPD provision in some of my previous schools has been delivered through external speakers and leadership during a twilight session. Let us just consider for a minute 'twilight sessions'. There were times when this session would fall on a day when I was timetabled to teach a full day as well as having a duty. The dangling carrot of these twilight sessions was the promise of an extra few days off in lieu of the end of the school academic year. Happy days! Although after a full day's teaching and a duty slot, the thought of sitting through two hours of training was not appealing. I wonder how much of the training I was actually able to absorb and take from it? In my current school these issues are alleviated with dedicated teacher development time every Friday. The school day finishes early for pupils and the rest of the afternoon is to support teacher education.

There has been a shift in recent years towards a more evidence-informed approach to teacher education. While I believe that this shift is a positive move for teacher education and agree that the role of using research-based evidence is important in improving teaching and learning there is a disconnect between 'talking about it' and the 'execution' of it (Nelson and Walker, 2019). Despite the introduction of online and face-to-face teacher CPD, such as researchED, there is still a discrepancy across the profession. In a report produced by Nelson and Walker (2019) for the National Foundation for Education Research on evidence-informed approaches to teaching some of the key findings were:

Key finding 1: Research evidence continues to play a relatively small role in influencing teachers' decision-making.
Teachers were much more likely to draw on their own experiences, or the experiences of other teachers/schools when making decisions about leadership or classroom practice than they were to use information produced by research organisations.
Key finding 2: Most teachers report that their schools offer supportive environments, which enable evidence-informed practice to flourish.
Despite the relatively small role played by research evidence in forming teachers' decision-making, our survey found that large proportions of teachers believed that their schools provided positive climates for professional learning and EIP.
Key finding 3: Teachers report generally positive attitudes towards research evidence.
Even though research evidence had only a small influence on teachers' decision making, teachers reported generally positive dispositions towards it.

The next step in teacher education is to provide the conditions in which teachers have the time to practice applying research into the classroom. Creating a culture where teachers have the autonomy and trust to use the research in their classrooms and work with other colleagues collaboratively to review the effectiveness of these strategies. The role of teacher coaching is something that already has a history dating back to the 1980s where Joyce and Showers began to highlight its benefits. They suggested that coaching, 'facilitates teachers' ability to translate knowledge and skills into actual classroom practice' (Kraft, Blazar and Hogan, 2018). This, for me, is the crucial element of teacher education. The investment in time to provide feedback to teachers that allows them to translate the knowledge and understanding of the research into the classroom. The Ambition Institute handbook on deliberate practice in teacher education shares the framework for facilitating practice in teacher development from Teacher Squared at Relay Graduate School of Education. The core thread that runs through their framework is building in the opportunity for teachers to spend time practising and colleagues providing feedback.

A framework for facilitating practice in teacher development

Are your teachers practicing? The right stuff?	Is your facilitation of practice high-quality	Is your facilitation making teachers more skilled?
Practice Happens	**Practice Shines**	**Practice Matters**
First... • Commit to practice • Protect planned practice *Then...* • Prioritise what to practice • Align goal & practice type	• Cultivate a culture of practice • Deliver practice • Frame • Model • Protocol • Close • Provide feedback on practice	• Data from practice session • Data from implementation
Every session should have aligned, meaningful practice and that time should be held sacred.	*Quality practice is meticulously planned and fastidiously enacted.*	*Practice only matters if teachers are becoming more skilled on-site and in their classrooms.*

For example, showing teachers how to improve the contribution of pupils answering questions through cold call is only the first step. There is a good probability that if they leave a training session, after some training on using cold calling for questioning, that not all teachers will apply it in their classroom. This could be for several reasons, perhaps they don't fully understand how to apply, or the reasons for applying it, or they don't feel comfortable in giving it a go. There's also the trap of 'I've always done it this way and it's worked for me, so I don't need to make any changes to my practice'. For the teachers that may choose to 'have a go' the quality of cold calling may not be in an effective way. This is because, when sharing new strategies for teachers to use, we need to build in time for them to create their own questions and practise using them. There have been many times when I've left a training session with a dozen formative assessment strategies that I could use in the classroom. The first decision is which one of these strategies should I use and then how I should go about trialling one of these strategies. Too often, teachers become overwhelmed by the number of strategies and this leads to none of them being tried. Effective teacher education requires the 'buy-in' from teachers and their commitment in wanting to practise, to improve so that practice happens.

3.3 The observation

I suspect that there are many teachers, including myself, who have experienced the dread of someone coming to observe your lesson, as Tom described at the start of this chapter. The problem with many of these observations is they are a means in which to create evidence for senior leaders to prove that teachers are either performing or not performing to their desired expectations. As Chris Moyse has passionately spoken about over the last few years, to create a collaborative and supportive culture schools would benefit from adopting an 'improve not prove' strategy when approaching teacher education. This will create the 'kind environments' that allow for the professional growth of teachers.

The observation of teachers is an important element in supporting professional development. First and foremost, for these observations to be effective they should be high challenge, low threat. This means any pay progression or grading shouldn't be a part of this process. Teacher observations should be a mechanism in which teachers can both support other teachers to improve, as well as learning from the teacher you are observing. Observations are just one way we can provide support to teachers to develop but it shouldn't be seen as the only way.

Just like Dylan Wiliam commented during one of his presentations about the use of grades being a distractor for pupils to improve, this is the same for teachers. When we use grades to give feedback on teacher observations, this is a distractor. Not to mention the validity of the grading that teachers have been awarded in the past. What one observer believed to be an outstanding lesson, another observer may grade the lesson satisfactory. Lesson grading is a subjective process and one that is usually based on the pre-conceived set of teaching principles that are similar to that of the observer.

'In order to get a rating of a teacher as reliable as the SAT, it turns out that you would need to see each teacher teaching six different classes and have each lesson rated by five independent judges. In other words, you would need 30 independent ratings of a teacher's performance to get a reliable rating of how good he or she is, and even that doesn't tell us whether the teacher is actually any good or not. We need 30 ratings just a get a reliable rating.'

If we genuinely want to improve teacher education and we want to use lesson observations as part of that process, we must see them as non-judgemental in relation to gradings. Prior to the observation, it is essential to establish the focus for the observation to best support the teacher being observed. This pre-observation discussion is both important for the observer and the teacher being observed. It determines the area of professional growth that the observation will be used to support the teacher to improve upon.

Whilst establishing the focus of the observation, use this time to discuss with the teacher how they want to receive their feedback. Throughout this book, I have demonstrated through the evidence indicated in the research the power of feedback when you cultivate the right conditions. Making teachers feel comfortable in receiving the feedback is important and, therefore, allowing the teacher to decide *how* they want to receive their feedback is a vital cog to ensure the feedback that the observer provides is well received. If the feedback being delivered is done in a way that does not support the receivers preferred format, this will ultimately result in the feedback being rejected. This will not help support the professional growth of colleagues.

When I asked teachers whether they have received their feedback in their preferred format, the results indicated that this often does not happen. The results showed 46% of teachers said they have received feedback in a format they have been unhappy with.

I have received feedback in a format that I have not been happy with.

429 responses

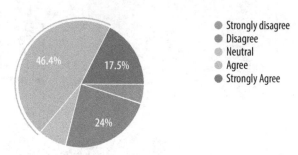

I asked teachers to reflect on their experiences of being observed. Some of the reflections can be read below:

'It was at lunchtime when I had a full day of teaching with meeting after school. I asked if I could quickly have the headlines and then more detailed feedback the next day. I was told no, and all of my lunchtime was taken up.'

'It was straight after a lesson, whilst my next class were waiting outside the door.'

'Immediately after. First question is always "how do you think the lesson went?", without having had time to reflect and settle down after the lesson. Observations are always nerve-wracking and feedback immediately after is not my preference.'

'When feedback has been given at an inappropriate time where there isn't a large enough time frame to adequately discuss, then feedback does not feel helpful because it is dumped on me, with no chance to collaboratively create actionable points for the future.'

These reflections illustrate some of the difficulties associated with the process of observations. As fellow colleagues, we should carefully consider the impact that feedback can have on others.

To avoid these difficulties, allow teachers to choose their preferred format for receiving this feedback during the initial discussion along with the intended focus. The clarity on the intended focus is important for the observer and the teacher. This preference could be shared at the start of the academic year and could be achieved through a professional teacher education portrait. This would be completed by a teacher at the beginning of the academic year to support building a collaborative culture. The teacher would identify how they would prefer to receive their feedback and would indicate their focus. This would allow staff to have autonomy over the feedback they receive and provide a clear focus on prioritising meaningful practice and quality feedback to improve.

The alternative example that follows, devised by Chris Moyse, allows teachers to share their focus in a prominent place in their classroom. This means when an observer walks into the classroom, they can provide concise feedback to the teacher on their particular focus at that moment in time. For example, a teacher could be focusing on improving their use of modelling.

Teachers are also learners

I am currently focusing on...

_____

_____

_____

3.4 Observing a lesson

For the observer, the power in the feedback you can provide to the teacher will be determined by the ability to share concrete examples of the different stages of the lesson. This is where the use of pre-determined observation sheets are a distraction and a plain piece of paper to make your notes will be more than sufficient and allow for you to capture the events that take place in the lesson.

At this point it is worth reflecting on Professor Coe's suggestion of poor proxies (Didau, 2015) for learning which he identified as follows:

1. Students are busy; lots of work is done, especially written work.
2. Students are engaged, interested, motivated.
3. Students are getting attention, feedback, explanations.
4. Classroom is ordered, clam, under control.
5. Curriculum has been 'covered', i.e. presented to students in some form.

6. At least some students have supplied correct answers whether they have really understood them or could reproduce them independently.

Therefore, when observing lessons, we should be aware of these poor proxies and, as Coe suggested, a more effective way of thinking about learning is 'when people have to think hard' (Didau, 2015). Of course, saying to a colleague that you observed pupils 'thinking hard' means nothing and is – as we already discussed at the beginning of this section on observations – very subjective, providing limited help for the teacher to improve. So, we should spend time looking for concrete examples of pupils thinking hard from the directions of the teacher. The most effective way of doing this is to record what the teacher and pupil say to capture the 'key moments' in the lesson that demonstrate when the teacher ignites the flame to encourage pupils to think hard. This could be during teacher explanation to capture how the teacher explains the concepts and processes being learned or the types of questions asked. Alongside this, record what the pupils say as they respond to the teacher's directions.

3.5 The observation feedback

Sharing lesson feedback with colleagues can be challenging, especially if they have not had a positive experience previously. When we have a negative experience – no matter what the context – we grow cautious of being subjected to that experience again. This is because the feedback we receive can lead to three triggers: truth triggers, relationship triggers and identity triggers outlined by Stone and Deen (2014). Firstly, we can be triggered by the context of the feedback itself. For lesson observations, this can often occur when the receiver does not agree or believe the observer's comments about their lesson. Secondly, the relationship we have with the person providing the feedback can have a trigger. If we feel the person giving us the feedback has a personal grudge against us, then the focus of the conversation will shift. The final trigger, identity triggers, is all about who we are. This is where the approach to any teacher education is important, especially if observations form part of this process. If we feel the lesson didn't go well, we can become overwhelmed and anxious to receive the feedback. Allowing the teacher to decide how and when they want to receive feedback is important, thus avoiding the possibility of derailing the subsequent conversation and not providing support for the receiver or the giver of the feedback.

If we want teachers to embrace the feedback, they need to understand it. There is a difference between listening to the feedback you are being given and understanding what it means. Feedback to teachers is often too generic with little substance to enable the receiver to understand it. Take the following examples of this generic feedback which follows.

'You need to have more clarity in how you explain ideas to students.'

'You need to work on improving the culture of learning in your classroom.'

'You need to question students more.'

'You need to differentiate for the ablest.'

'You need to work on improving your presence in the classroom.'

I'm sure there have been times when you have received this generic feedback and, in many cases, received multiple generic feedback targets to work on. Similar to what we discussed in chapter 2 on the role of feedback to pupils, when the feedback is too vague this makes it difficult to understand. For example, what do we mean by 'you need more clarity in how you explain' or what does it mean to 'improve the culture of learning'. If the feedback is not clear this will make it difficult for the receiver to process and know how to improve their practice.

All these points need unravelling further, they need to be more granular so that there is a clear understanding of what it means to improve the culture of learning. It might be that, as an observer, you feel that the highest leverage action for that teacher is the climate for learning however, this part of pedagogy is huge and there are so many variables that underpin this part of teaching. Therefore, when feeding back to teachers we should provide the specific guidance on the next steps that will contribute towards the building blocks to support improvement. Here are some examples of how this might look when feedback is given to colleagues. The graphic organisers, created by David Goodwin, illustrate how observers can breakdown the next steps for teachers using some of Doug Lemov's 'Teach Like A Champion' techniques. The following graphic organisers focus on a climate for learning, questioning and feedback.

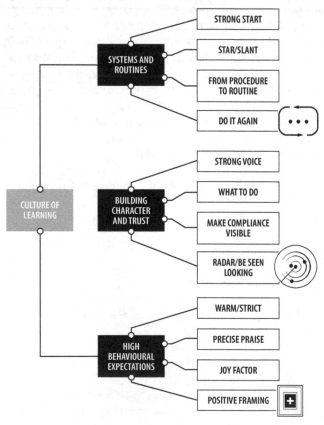

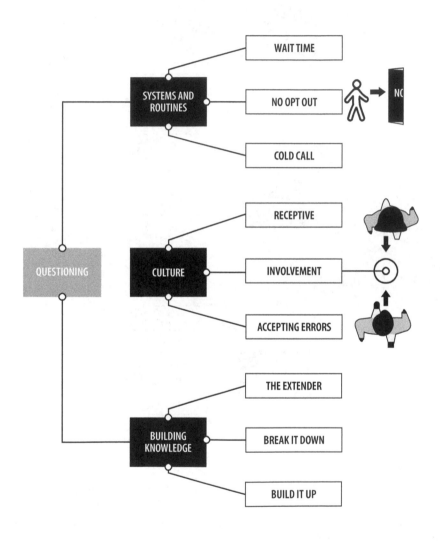

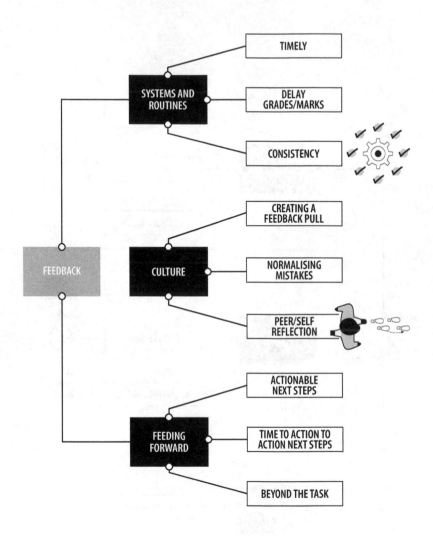

The following WalkThru on the adjacent page provides an overview of how an observer could approach the lesson feedback and the follow up support with a teacher. In the next spotlight, Sam Gibbs provides further insight on how instructional coaching can be a powerful tool to support teacher education.

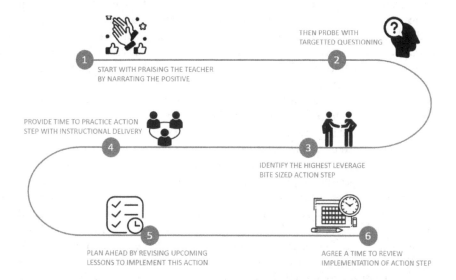

1. START WITH PRAISING THE TEACHER BY NARRATING THE POSITIVE

2. THEN PROBE WITH TARGETED QUESTIONING

3. IDENTIFY THE HIGHEST LEVERAGE BITE SIZED ACTION STEP

4. PROVIDE TIME TO PRACTICE ACTION STEP WITH INSTRUCTIONAL DELIVERY

5. PLAN AHEAD BY REVISING UPCOMING LESSONS TO IMPLEMENT THIS ACTION

6. AGREE A TIME TO REVIEW IMPLEMENTATION OF ACTION STEP

Teacher Spotlight: Teacher education through coaching

SAM GIBBS, REGIONAL TUTOR FOR AMBITION INSTITUTE

Sam has taught English in secondary schools across West Yorkshire for 12 years. She works as a regional tutor for Ambition Institute, supporting schools across the North of England with evidence-based approaches to training and coaching. Sam is co-founder of English-Ed (www.english-ed.co.uk) which works with English departments on curriculum design and implementation and delivers subject-specific training and coaching. She is a governor at a local primary school. You can find her tweeting as @Samlgibbs1

During my NQT year, I was observed teaching my Year 7 English class by the deputy head of the school. It was high-stakes and I was nervous but prepared. The lesson plan was printed, the worksheets were differentiated in three ways, the card sort was laminated. Towards the end of the lesson, the observer caught my eye, nodded, smiled and left the room. It had gone well, I thought. The pupils had behaved, I'd got through my lesson plan and I'd remembered to follow the school policy on rewarding pupils' answers with stamps.

The following day, I received my feedback via my staff pigeon hole. It was an A3 sheet, divided into the four Ofsted grading criteria, littered with ticks to show which I had achieved in the lesson. At the bottom of the page, the words 'Target: extend the top end' were written. I was left confused. I had given the pupils marked on my register as 'Gifted and Talented' a separate worksheet, with two extension tasks – what more could I have done? This type of feedback was typical of the kind I received for most of my teaching career. It was almost always recorded against Ofsted or school performance criteria and used to determine my progression. Any targets I was set for improvement were usually taken from the criteria above the one I had been deemed to have achieved. Often, I had no idea how to achieve them, because there was no follow-up to the lesson observation. I assumed I would improve with time and experience, and so, perhaps, did my observers.

Later in my career, when I had gained 'Advanced Skills Teacher' status, I was rarely observed at all. There seemed to be an assumption that I must be good and so not only did I not need feedback on my own teaching practice but I was now somehow qualified to give it to others. The last time I was observed, I had gone three years without anyone coming into my classroom for the purposes of providing feedback to me. The head of history came to see me teach my Year 10 top set as part of a trial of the lesson study method the school was considering rolling out. In our feedback conversation, she was clearly embarrassed and told me that she realised 'of course, I don't need to give you any targets – the lesson was great!' The target recorded on her observation sheet was that, should a bell ring to signal a minute silence (on this occasion, for Armistice Day) I should try to link the content of my lesson more clearly to the reason for the bell. I had been teaching duality in 'Jekyll and Hyde' – the links did not seem obvious.

Both types of feedback left me equally frustrated. Targets which highlighted what I hadn't done, but not how to do it, left me feeling not good enough. But nor did I want false flattery, or even genuine flattery. I just wanted to understand how I could get better.

In my work with teachers across the country I hear frequently that they don't receive regular feedback on their teaching practice, that feedback they do receive is tied to performance and accountability systems, and where they are given targets there is not usually guidance in how to apply them. I strongly believe that all teachers want and should strive to improve their practice – not, as Dylan Wiliam (NWEAvideos, 2012) states, because we are not already good enough – but because we can all be even better.

When we talk about feedback in education we usually mean for pupils. But we know that the biggest driver for improving pupil outcomes is the quality of teaching that they receive. It stands to reason that we need to focus our attention on supporting our teachers to keep getting better. The quality of feedback they receive has a direct impact on the life chances of their pupils – it shouldn't be a lottery based on a teacher's school context or the generosity of their colleagues.

Instructional coaching differs from the types of feedback teachers habitually receive, because the observation is just one part of a continuing cycle of development, rather than the episodic kind I received in the early years of my career, and because the feedback is very precise. Sam Sims (2019) defines instructional coaching as 'an expert teacher working with a novice in an individualised, classroom-based, observation-feedback-practice cycle'. The coach observes the teacher for a short 10 to 15-minute period, then sets an action step designed to move their practice incrementally forwards. In the coaching conversation which follows, the coach provides a clear model for the teacher of how they can achieve the action step, facilitates deliberate practice and provides specific, high-quality feedback on the teacher's performance. The action steps are very focused but build to have a powerful impact on the teacher's practice over time.

Key active ingredients of effective instructional coaching:

1. **One action step**
   An action step needs to be so specific and precise that a teacher can implement it immediately. At the same time, a skilled coach recognises that the lesson observed is only a proxy for understanding the teacher's current level of practice and has an eye on the bigger picture. Coaching is a journey of development which unfolds over time.

2. **Cycle of model, deliberate practice, feedback**
   A coach plans and delivers a model of better, to show the teacher the difference between their current practice and the desired state. The teacher is then able to put the action step into practice in the coaching session and receive immediate feedback from their coach. The coach increases the complexity of the practice as necessary to move the teacher forward, providing continuous feedback for improvement which precisely and specifically shows the next steps. The cycle of model, practice, feedback supports learning and development incrementally over time: what works for pupils works for adults too.

3. **Building trusting relationships**
   Successful coaching is built upon a trusting relationship between teacher and coach. For this reason, coaching should be non-judgemental and non-evaluative, and should not be tied to school performance management systems. Its purpose is not to tick things off a checklist. Performativity and accountability systems have been as damaging to teachers as they have to pupils: my experience has been that many teachers bring the baggage of

more punitive observation systems to coaching and can understandably be quite defensive at first. Some respond very emotionally to feedback. I can recall one teacher who burst into tears when I praised an aspect of her lesson and told me it was the first time in ten years someone had told her something she was doing was good. Acknowledging prior experiences is important to building trust and mutual respect and to getting the best out of a coachee. For a coach to be able to establish a culture for practice and feedback, a teacher needs to feel safe and comfortable.

Subsequently, choosing the right people to coach is of the utmost importance. They need to have the credibility and emotional intelligence to get buy-in from teachers. They need to be able to listen, to unpick, to work out where teachers are at, to understand what their concerns are, to consider if they are the right concerns. Crucially, they also need to be able to invest the time. Consistency and routine are key. For the teacher, the coaching session is their space to prioritise their development, and the time for it must be protected.

Implementing instructional coaching successfully across a school takes careful consideration and planning. It takes time to become a skilled coach. An expert coach has a high level of conscious competence: they can break down their expertise into granular components and plan a sequence of learning for a novice to support them in building mental models. As such, training and continuous professional development for coaches should be a key part of any coaching programme and embedded in a culture of wider learning in a school.

Teachers are extremely busy people with an incredibly demanding job. They have a million things to think about and, amongst all of those things, they will always put themselves and their development last. As a coach, your job is to put it first. Teachers deserve the same time, effort and expertise put into them as they give to their pupils.

3.6 Departmental feedback

The notion of teachers practising pedagogy in front of their peers may be daunting and sharing their practice with others may create a feeling of vulnerability. These feelings will vary dependent upon the experience of the teacher. It might be that the very idea of an experienced teacher practising with an NQT and receiving feedback on a particular aspect of pedagogy may be seen as something that wouldn't be of benefit to them. We talked earlier about the three feedback triggers and one of these relating to the relationships we have with people. For example, what we may believe about NQTs, they are not as experienced as someone who has been teaching for a while, therefore how can they provide me with feedback that I can learn from?

This is where the building a culture of practice in schools where receiving feedback is beneficial for all is important to establish. Practising in smaller groups within departments can be beneficial to support the increased use of teacher practice.

The following spotlight explores the power of teachers sharing feedback on observations of a learner in their lessons, intending to reduce exclusions in mainstream secondary schools.

Specialist Spotlight: 'Early Intervention: Reducing Exclusions'

The Mulberry Bush School is an outstanding, non-maintained residential special school and children's home providing specialist residential therapeutic care, treatment and education for traumatised children aged 5-13 and their families from across England and Wales. For this project, Mulberry Bush Outreach and Oxfordshire School Inclusion Team were commissioned to work with several mainstream secondary schools with high levels of fixed-term and permanent exclusions.

An aim of the 'Early Intervention: Reducing Exclusions' project is to encourage early identification of pupils as they started to show signs of not coping with school. The model of the project is rooted in recognising the impact of trauma and early life attachment difficulties. Throughout the project, Mulberry Bush staff encouraged school-based staff to become more self-reflective and supported staff in recognising their own emotional responses to pupils' behaviour and how to manage this better. Collaboration between staff is strongly promoted so that pupils experience a consistent response from the whole team. A senior leader is trained in the approach as a part of the project so that the intervention can continue after the project ended.

Throughout the project, which includes a whole staff training and two clinic sessions, Mulberry Bush staff model a way of working for school staff. In this specific case study, the project structure was repeated four times throughout the year, each time focusing on a different pupil that the school had identified as being at risk of exclusion. Each of the four cycles included:

- Twilight training session for all staff: Mulberry Bush staff shared data about the profile of pupils who are most likely to be excluded and the most common behaviour that leads to exclusions.

- Comprehensive pupil profile: the pupil profile brings together all of the most important information about the pupil including their early life experiences, any specific strengths or difficulties that affected their learning, what aspects of school life they found hard or easy.
- First clinic: an hour session which included every member of staff who worked with the pupil. Mulberry Bush staff facilitated the clinic so that everyone, in turn, talked about their experience of working with the pupil and what emotional impact this was having on them. Mulberry Bush staff created a safe space where staff would not feel judged or criticised for sharing difficulties or negative feelings they were experiencing. During this time all staff were encouraged to listen carefully to each other. The last 20 minutes of the session was allocated to reflect on what was heard and what staff felt this told them about when the pupil was able to learn and relate well to others, and what led to things becoming difficult. In the last part of the clinic, staff agreed on some consistent strategies and responses.
- Second clinic: this clinic took place six weeks later, in a similar format as the first clinic. Again, each member of staff, in turn, spoke about the pupil. In this meeting, there was a greater emphasis on what changes each member of staff had noticed, which time at the end of the clinic again allocated for reflection and agreeing what should be done next to support the pupil.

The project encouraged collaborative working, where staff were feeding back to each other about their experiences working with a pupil at risk of exclusion. Through sharing their experiences, staff were able to reflect on their individual experiences and determine strategies to deploy to support the learner. The impact of the project was evidenced at both a whole school and an individual level.

At the whole-school level

School 1:
'Team around the Child' is now embedded practice. Clinics are scheduled into the directed time budget. These happen every half term and focus upon the child with the highest need at that time. The criteria for these include increased incidence of poor behaviours, or potentially decreasing attendance and reduced engagement, all of which impacts upon their progress and potentially those around them.

All teachers who teach the child gather and share feelings, successes and barriers/frustrations. This provides the opportunity for colleagues to share in a supportive environment their experiences. The group then problem solve and identify a shared strategy. This is then shared with the child by the team captain (usually the person who knows the child best). This is one of the most powerful elements of the process for us as the child knows that staff have all invested their time to help them.

After six weeks the core team, team captain, behaviour coordinator and myself re-group to evaluate. If things are progressing in the right direction we continue, if things need to be tweaked, we recall the whole team to brainstorm again. Over time, the vast majority of students who have been involved in this approach have improved and remain active participants in their education. Where we have not experienced success, we would expect this is usually due to external environmental factors.

The power for the staff is the united support of colleagues with the same student, the early warning if one lesson has not gone well, the email giving the heads up, provides the forewarned forearmed strategy. Our change in language and the emphasis that behaviour is communication is changing the ethos of the school.

School 2:
The project has been influential in developing our inclusive practice within our school. A concept that we initially thought quite simple grew to be very powerful in developing in-class provision. The initial consultation with parents to develop a comprehensive profile gave staff a deeper understanding of the students. Staff felt this was so important that we have now introduced a weekly safeguarding/student information briefing.

The comprehensive profile must be well thought out and careful consideration of the appropriateness of information being shared, although it may be sensitive it did influence staff behaviours. From this, we found staff sometimes were making excuses. These staff responses need challenging, using evidence to support impact does help but what also helps is explaining they have the skills the students do not yet possess.

Using the model to find a common approach was hugely successful. It empowered staff, made them feel confident in taking the provision away and trying to implement it in their classrooms. This year we have seen a huge shift in staff going out of their way to develop their relationships with students. They can no longer pass the responsibility on to a different team to support.

One area we are focusing on is staff awareness and the level of knowledge the chair (in our case, myself and the SENCo) has to offer guidance and challenge. The approach will be dependent on the staffing but challenging their current practice is key to success.

We have loved the opportunity to work with the team and, hopefully, they are following through and doing the project justice.

Feedback from individual participants:

- '[This] has helped to lift staff groups who have felt defeated – [they have] recognised that their input can make such a difference.' – Welfare officer
- 'We now have a process for pupils we are struggling with, who we feel are at risk of exclusion. The framework and time has been of real benefit.' – SENCo
- 'It has enabled staff to respond to a wider range of pupils' needs.' – Deputy head

Key takeaways

- Teachers should feel supported, empowered and given the chance to develop into consciously competent practitioners that continually reflect on how they can support every pupil and their colleagues to succeed.
- Getting teacher education right in schools is important to the morale and wellbeing of teachers.
- When 'wicked' environments exist, this creates irrelevant and confusing feedback.
- Teacher observations should be a mechanism in which teachers can both support other teachers to improve, as well as learning from the teacher you are observing.
- If we genuinely want to improve teacher education, and we want to use lesson observations as part of that process, we must see them as non-judgemental concerning gradings.
- When feeding back to teachers we should provide the specific guidance on the next step that over time will contribute towards the building blocks to support their improvement.
- Practising in smaller groups within departments can be beneficial to support the increased use of teacher practice.

QR codes for chapter resources

 QUESTIONING WALK THRU CULTURE WALK THRU FEEDBACK WALK THRU

Chapter reflections

Use the space below to reflect on your own experiences of receiving feedback from colleagues.

Chapter 3 references

Department for Education (2019) 'Teacher recruitment and retention strategy'. London: The Stationery Office.

Department for Education (2018) 'School workforce in England: November 2017'. London: The Stationery Office.

Department for Education (2016) 'Schools workforce in England 2010 to 2015: trends and geographical comparisons'. London: The Stationery Office.

Didau, D. (2015) 'What might be a good proxy for learning?', *Learning Spy* [Online] 22 March. Retrieved from: www.bit.ly/38UdoRp

Evidence Based Education, Coe, R., Rauch, C. J., Kime, S. and Singleton, D. (2020) 'Great Teaching Toolkit: Evidence Review'. Retrieved from: www.bit.ly/3kJv0BL

Hogarth, R. M. (2001) *Educating Intuition*. Chicago: Chicago University Press.

Kraft, M. A., Blazar, D., Hogan, D. (2018) 'The effect of teaching coaching on instruction and achievement: A meta-analysis of the causal evidence', *Review of Educational Research* 88 (4) pp. 547-588.

Nelson, J. and Walker, M. (2019) 'Evidence-informed approaches to teaching – where are we now?', *National Foundation for Education Research* [Online] 13 May. Retrieved from: www.bit.ly/3pGyx7u

NWEAvideos (2012) 'Every Teacher Can Improve', *YouTube* [Video] 14 December. Retrieved from: www.bit.ly/3lIUUHa

Sims, S. (2019) 'Four reasons instructional coaching is currently the best-evidenced form of CPD', *Sam Sims Quantitative Education Research* [Online] 19 February. Retrieved from: www.bit.ly/33W8PTb

Stone, D. and Heen, S. (2014) *Thanks for the Feedback: The Science and Art of Receiving Feedback Well*. London: Penguin.

UCAS (2018) 'UTT monthly statistics: applicants'. Retrieved from: www.bit.ly/38PEDN3

4

FEEDBACK TO PARENTS: PROVIDING THE FOUNDATIONS TO TRIANGULATE THE FEEDBACK LOOP

'Schools and parents have a shared priority to deliver the best outcomes for their children.' – Education Endowment Foundation

Chapter checklist

✓ Invest time in communicating with parents to share the expectations.
✓ Share the role parents can have in supporting their child to achieve.
✓ Create regular lines of communication with parents to share their child's learning journey throughout the academic year.
✓ Establish opportunities to share with parents their child's progress in subjects.
✓ Equip and empower parents to know how they can create regular study routines and the role they can play in supporting their child in learning at home.
✓ The active role of parents in supporting their child's learning demonstrates a positive correlation with outcomes.
✓ The effectiveness of parental engagement varies with limited evidence on the most effective strategies to improve engagement.

4.1 Parental engagement vs parental partnership

A tale of two different scenarios…

Tom, a Year 11 pupil, is dreading next week as the annual parents' evening looms. For the last four years, he has sat through some of the most uncomfortable experiences of his years. He knows that his teachers will inform his parents that he isn't performing as well as he should be and that his behaviour isn't meeting the expected standard. He knows that this message will be echoed by most of his teachers. However, the one saving grace is Miss Thornton, his English teacher, because she has been teaching him since Year 9 and always gives his parents positive feedback. This is the lesson he feels he is achieving best in. Tom knows that after parents' evening he will be told by his parents he needs to knuckle down and will end up losing his pocket money for the next few weeks. His mum and dad know they need to support him somehow but they are not sure where to start.

Abigail, a Year 10 pupil, really looks forward to parents' evening every year. It's a great opportunity for her parents to hear about how well she is doing in all of her subjects. She knows that her parents will be given a positive report from all of her teachers about how well she behaves in lessons and that she always tries her best. It has become an expectation that her parents always say to her we know exactly what they are going to say about you. Her tutor, Mr Butcher always wraps up the evening by saying, 'Well, I bet it has been a really positive evening tonight, as it always is.' She leaves parents' evening with her parents extremely proud of her and they love to tell her grandparents about the positive reports she receives during the evening. Abi's parents leave knowing she is doing well but the reasons behind her success, how she could improve and what they can do as parents to support her to make these improvements are not so clear.

The Education Endowment Foundation's guidance report (2018) on working with parents to support children's learning indicates the crucial role parents play in supporting their child's learning. The report suggests four key recommendations to consider when working with parents.

- **Recommendation 1:** critically review how you work with parents.
- **Recommendation 2:** provide practical strategies to support learning at home.
- **Recommendation 3:** tailor school communications to encourage positive dialogue about learning.
- **Recommendation 4:** offer more sustained and intensive support where needed.

Despite the positive correlation between parental involvement and pupil outcomes, the degree to which parents and schools engage effectively in supporting children along their learning journey varies considerably due to the demand on parents' time. Janet Goodall and Caroline Montgomery (2014) outlined the move from parental involvement to parental engagement, leading to an effective partnership between school and home. Just like the two scenarios of Tom and Abigail demonstrate the degree to which parents are involved in their child's schooling varies, there is a difference between being involved and being engaged. This is where Goodall and Montgomery present a model to demonstrate the progression from parental involvement to engagement with children's learning. The model that is illustrated below represents the different stages schools may move between from being involved to being engaged with their child's learning.

	Parental involvement with schools	
Parents' evening	Reading with children	Parental interventions
Parents passive recipients of information	In school – school directed, 'helping teacher'	School led, little or no parental involvement in setting up or running
	Parental involvement with schooling	
Parents' evening	Reading with children	Parental interventions
Dialogue between parents and staff	In school, some parental discretion	Jointly planned and led by parents, after consultation
	Parental engagement with children's learning	
Parents' evening	Reading with children	Parental interventions
Parent-led discussion of teaching and learning	Not in school, parent and child led	Parent devised and led

The model represents the concept of seeing engagement as a continuum, something that is happening continually and is not something for schools to merely 'tick' off a list and considered 'done' because each new academic year brings new cohorts of parents. Children change as they age, and parental engagement with their learning needs to adapt to these changes (Goodall and Montgomery, 2014). When there is a partnership between home and school this can contribute towards boosting children's self-esteem and increasing their motivation towards learning. Despite this positive correlation, the EEF report indicated that in the majority of schools there isn't an explicit plan for engaging with parents and fewer than 10% of teachers receive guidance on how to engage with parents.

In many schools the feedback parents receive from teachers is often in the format of information giving. Take a typical academic year, parents will receive countless letters from a variety of teachers, ranging from the standard half-termly update from the headteacher to the notification of an upcoming field trip from the geography department. Alongside the communication from letters, there will be the yearly parents' evening, written reports and the occasional phone calls home to update when a child may be a cause for concern or to praise them for going above and beyond. A lot of this communication to parents is giving information that is predominantly controlled by the school rather than information being actively sought by parents. This is an example of the difference between 'involvement' and 'engagement' in their child's learning. To enhance feedback given to parents about their child we need to move from giving information to parents actively seeking out information about their child. The feedback should be a two-way process that is happening continually throughout the academic year to allow a strong partnership to form.

In the next section, I will unpick how we can use parents' evening as a consolidation of discussing a child's progress rather than, in some cases, it being the main point of discussion about the progress a child has made during the academic year.

4.2 Parents' evenings and generating GROW conversations

The example of Tom and Abigail at the beginning of the chapter highlight some of the historical issues that I have witnessed and been a part of when it comes to the annual parents' evening. There are often two types of parents' evening that can unfold. Tom's example illustrates the first type that occurs where the pupil has proved challenging throughout the academic year and, inevitably, the parents' evening turns into the parents being told that their child is underperforming, which leaves them disappointed with their child. These types of evenings can be quite challenging, especially if you have had a difficult relationship with a pupil.

I have experienced it before where you just know as the parents sit down that their child has prepped them for slightly more negative feedback about their behaviour and progress. They have informed their parents how you 'pick on them' and single them out. The parents are ready for this showdown. These are the kind of appointments that catch you off guard and leave you feeling like it's your fault because it turns into parents giving you feedback on how your relationship with their child is part of your personal crusade to not like their child. Even worse, these appointments are the ones that lead to a backlog of appointments and you inevitably find yourself the last one standing.

When I think back to my training and NQT years there was little advice about parents' evenings. It was just 'come and watch and see how it's done'. Inevitably, I watched on as my mentor did his parents' evening and he allowed me to pitch in with my thoughts for any shared groups we had during my training year. By the time I was an NQT it was expected that I would know how to do a parents' evening. The problem is that a parents' evening is an opportunity to give parents information about their child but only late in the year, information that really should have been discussed earlier. There are, of course, those parents who you have forged a relationship with and this is a good opportunity to catch up and tell them that their child is doing really well, they're on target, and you really enjoy teaching them. These are the quick and easy appointments, where you have little to say. As time went on and I did more and more parents' evenings, I started to develop a script. One for a pupil who was doing well and another for a pupil who was not. The more I reflect I realise that this feedback was too generic and more about giving information to parents, hoping that they will be supportive and echo your concerns if their child needs to make improvements to achieve.

Moving forward in our use of parents' evenings, there is an opportunity to create more effective GROW conversations to shift from parental involvement to a greater emphasis on forming a partnership with parents to triangulate the feedback loop. The GROW coaching model was first developed by Sir John Whitmore and colleagues at Performance Consultants International during the 1980s with the main aim to provide a more effective way to create stronger leaders. The GROW model is now a widely recognised approach to coaching that is used worldwide by businesses to improve performance.

G – GOAL	R – REALITY	O – OPTIONS	W – WAY FORWARD
(Aspirations)	**(Current obstacles or situations)**	**(Strengths, resources)**	**(Accountability and personal actions)**
Share with parents what the aspirations are for their child within your subject. For example, identifying a specific area that would enable them to move forward but not merely discussing their target grade.	Discuss the current obstacles that are in the way for their child to achieve the main goal. This could be related to behaviour for learning, completion of homework to consolidate understanding, or developing a particular skill.	At this point, it is what their child needs to do overcome the obstacles and achieve the goal.	An opportunity to set the targets for the coming weeks both with pupils and provide parents with the tools in which to support the options for moving forward.

Prior to this conversation, allow pupils to choose their 'best' piece of work to share. This will provide an opportunity for them to discuss why they feel this is their best piece of work and allow parents to understand their own child's thought process. The potential move to online consultations means these could be gathered through Google Classroom and shared on screen during the consultation.

4.3 Reporting

I can't even begin to imagine the number of hours I have spent writing the annual reports. I have long wondered their effectiveness as a form of communicating with parents versus the amount of time invested in them by schools. It's not just the process of writing them that takes time, but the quality assurance checks they go through at different stages before being sent home. The originality of these reports has also changed over time. Reading back over my original reports from school, my teachers had written their reports by hand and they had a feel of authenticity about them. Reading them makes me feel that this is about me and how well I have done. In contrast, today's reports are often generated from comment banks, copied and pasted with minor tweaks to reflect the different levels of commitment and progress by pupils.

Specialist Spotlight: Parental feedback to pupils with ASC

RACHEL FOX, SPECIALIST TEACHER

Rachel Cox is a specialist SEND teacher for Warwickshire Country Council. You can find her tweeting as @_RachelCox

All families deserve open and honest feedback about their child's progress, and this is no different for families of children who have Autism Spectrum Condition (ASC). In the classroom, children with ASC can face daily challenges that neurotypical children do not due to their differences with social communication and interaction and also their repetitive and restrictive behaviours, which include differences in sensory regulation. These differences can have a huge impact on the child's academic progress, which then leads to the need for challenging conversations between teachers and families to provide sensitive feedback that may be difficult to hear. Nevertheless, no matter how challenging this conversation may be for both parties, it must take place as soon as possible so that the child can receive the support that they require and they can begin to learn strategies to assist them with the challenges they face.

Working as an advisory teacher often means that challenging conversations with families regarding feedback that their child is having difficulties coping in the classroom, with either academic, social interaction or communication demands, have often already happened. However, this does not mean that this makes my role any easier when my involvement with a child requires feedback to families about observations and assessments that I have carried out. Often families, quite rightly so, want answers and quick fixes when it comes to providing support for their child around the difficulties their child may be facing. Yet quick fixes are not possible so, inevitably, feedback given to families needs to be realistic and empowering for them but at the same time sympathetic and personalised. Having worked as a teacher in both mainstream and special primary schools, I appreciate that I have often spent time building relationships with families in various ways.

Consequently, providing any feedback – positive or negative – seems to be somewhat easier as the foundations of trust and respect have already been put in place. This is not the case at all with my current role as an advisory teacher. Often providing feedback to families from observations and assessments I have conducted with their child is the first time that I have had contact with them. So it is essential that feedback is carefully thought out and that there are other professionals present and involved, such as the SENCO, class teacher and teaching assistant. This ensures that everyone is working together as a team around the child to ensure the best possible outcomes for them.

As part of the advisory teacher role, a written report is completed after any observation or assessment, which is structured in a way that also enables constructive verbal feedback to be delivered to families. Any feedback delivered is always started by providing a context as to why I been asked to observe the child, including where, when and why. For example, 'I have been asked to observe Johnny on the playground because there are concerns that he is finding it difficult to interact with his peers at playtimes.' After giving a context, discussions would take place around what I saw during my observations or assessments. This feedback would be focused on facts and the actual behaviours that I saw (using the earlier example), during the playtimes that I feel impact on Johnny making successful interactions with his peers.

I would avoid any feedback on the child's personality or character to avoid the parents becoming defensive and losing any opportunity for a meaningful feedback session. Possible reasons as to why the behaviours I observed may be occurring would then be fed back. Here I would consider the emotional impact that this would be having on the child and the significance of this. The final stage of the feedback at this point would be to look at the support that can be put in place to enable the child to be successful. This support must be personalised. To do this, I would be using all of my knowledge about the child's likes and strengths and include them in any suggested strategies. These are aspects that I would have picked up on and asked the child about during observations and/or assessments. The feedback given during this part of the process should empower the families and give a clear plan of what support that not only the school are going to put in place, but how the families themselves can be involved to ensure their child is successful and making progress. At this stage of the feedback process, it would be agreed on how further feedback is going to be given. This may look very different for each individual and when a child is facing challenges in the classroom that go beyond academia, it may be more appropriate to have more frequent contact with families, provide more regular feedback and have more frequent reviews. This may be in the form of a half-termly review, a daily diary or email where feedback on significant achievements for that child can be recognised, or even a 'wow' book where pictures and work are regularly set home for the children to share with their families. These are all very different forms of feedback but equally as effective. It is important to remember that what might be a small piece of feedback for one child and their family may be a significant piece of feedback for others, they may have been waiting to hear it for a long time. So remember no achievement is too small, every achievement is worth feeding back to families.

In addition to this, non-academic feedback is just as important, if not more important than providing academic feedback, especially for children with ASC who have social interaction and communication differences. Maslow before Bloom is a huge topic of conversation at the moment and, in my own experience, I know that families of children with ASC value feedback on how their child has managed emotionally or socially during their day at school, as much or even more than 'they wrote a fantastic piece of writing in English today'. To conclude, I will return to one of my first points: no matter how hard feedback may be to deliver to families, you must be open and honest and see it as an opportunity to empower parents and allow them to become a partner in their child's progress. Time needs to be taken to structure feedback carefully and delivering it effectively takes practice but it is worth investing the time as the results can be extremely positive.

Specialist Spotlight: Engaging families living with complexity in their child's progress

PEN GREEN CHILDREN'S CENTRE

In July 2004 Pen Green Children's Centre opened The Baby and Toddler Nest, a provision for children from nine months to three years old. The provision has 15 full-time places and is open 48 weeks of the year, from 8am to 6pm. The provision follows a constructivist pedagogy with reflective practitioners, supporting children to be autonomous learners and promoting children's sense of agency. Pen Green also has a nursery space provision for three to five-year-olds. Practitioners, alongside the SENDCo and SEN support worker collaborate with parents and outside agencies to help early identification of SEN.

In working in partnership with parents and carers, the intention is to:

- try and gain a deeper understanding of a parent's perspective of having a child with complex needs.
- gain a greater understanding of how to work in close collaboration with the parent and other practitioners involved.
- understand and provide for the complex needs of a child.

To understand the child, staff at Pen Green:

- have conversations regularly with the parent/carers, including home visits and voice recorded interviews.
- undertake observations of the child in a 1:1 and small group setting.
- work in partnership with parents/carers, using parental observations in the home to inform their understanding of the child.
- share school-based observations with the parents/carers, staff working with the child and other professionals through a one-page profile.

To ensure consistency in staff gaining a thorough understanding of all learners with complexity, senior leaders ensure that all staff are competent in:

- writing a one-page profile that celebrates the child's strengths, identifies support needs and allows details to be shared.
- carrying out effective observations of a child's play, developing a vocabulary and skill base that recognises the subtle details in a child's behaviour that are indicators of a child engaged in, and learning from, their play experiences.

- creating a unique and whole picture of the child using Pen Green's framework.
- describing the child in terms of what they can do, and avoiding statements of what a child cannot do.

The Pen Green loop

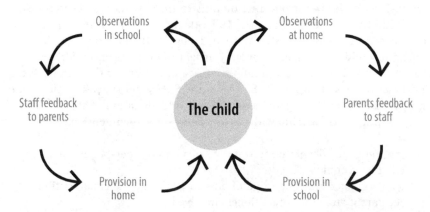

The relationship between the staff and parents is critical at every stage of a learner's journey. Initial home visits can start to build a trusting relationship, and ongoing visits can strengthen the dialogue between staff and parents/carers. In order to work in partnership with parents/carers, staff need to:

- see the parents/carers as the expert about the child.
- be sensitive to the whole family situation and consider things from the family's perspective.
- ask the right questions to gather the important facts and pertinent information about the child.
- engage in difficult conversations with parents, including learning skills linked with sharing difficult news.
- engage in reflective practice with parents/carers and colleagues to produce the best outcomes for children.

Close working relationships with parents enable staff to support families throughout the year before starting school. Practitioners and the SEN team follow the assess, plan, do review cycle and working alongside parents apply for additional funding and EHCP if required. Transition work includes close working with parents and outside agencies as well as developing relationships with local primary school SENCos and reception class teachers.

All parents of children with SEN are offered an in-depth transition meeting with the family worker and SEN team from Pen Green as well as the SENCo and reception teacher of the receiving primary school and any other outside agencies involved. Pen Green practitioners offer support for parents to complete EHCPs and apply for their chosen schools as well as opportunities for receiving schools to visit children in the setting.

'H is my son T's family worker, no words can describe the impact H has had on not only T's but my own life. She went above and beyond to help and support us going through his diagnosis and I will be forever grateful to her. H is still playing an active role in my son's diagnosis and helping to support me as a mother who doesn't have much support around her.'

To support staff in working in partnership with parents/carers, senior leaders need to ensure staff:

- have regular, planned 1:1 supervision in place.
- have access to individualised training and professional development.

When asked about the support and provision received at Pen Green, one parent stated, 'a lifeline for me during my most difficult times.' For further information about the provision in place at Pen Green, visit pengreen.org

4.4 Regular communication

One of the key areas we discussed at the start of this chapter was moving from involvement to partnership with our parents. In a research study, the communication parents receive from primary schools seems to suggest that parents feel more engaged with their child's education compared to when their child reaches secondary school (Williams, Williams and Ullman, 2002).

Involvement level		
	% of very involved parents	**% of less involved parents**
Selected child is at primary school	64%	54%
Selected child is a boy	52%	50%
Mum	65%	57%
Married couple	74%	75%
Parent finished education aged 16 or younger	53%	55%
Parent not working full time	59%	48%
More than one child aged 5-16	52%	54%
Base: all very involved (609), less involved (1410)		

This change in the involvement level as outlined by the research indicates that the likely reason for this is not about parents desire to be involved but a decline in their ability to be able to practically help their child as the complexity of the work their child does increases beyond primary education. This where modelling and supporting parents through the process is important at all stages of education, something I expand on in the next section. Alongside this support through modelling is also about regular communication with our parents throughout the academic year to provide them with clear feedback on their child's learning journey.

The challenge is to keep the line of communication open throughout the academic year so that the annual parents' evenings or written reports are not presented with any surprises. Many schools now communicate with parents regularly through text messages and emails to keep that line of communication open during the academic year. Feedback to parents through weekly phone calls can be an important way to build a rapport with parents of the pupils you teach. This could be phoning several parents at the end of the week to update them on their child's progress and how the parent could help to support their child moving forward in the coming weeks.

Making several phone calls each week to parents can be time-consuming and it won't allow you to reach out to all of the parents of the pupils you teach. An alternative to maintain an open dialogue with parents and share feedback on their child's progress in your subject is to encourage pupils to take home their class books each half term to promote an open discussion between parent and child on what they have been learning.

4.5 Modelling

In the previous chapters, we have discussed the role of modelling and practice as important elements of establishing an effective feedback culture. There can be a tendency to assume that parents know how to support their child in learning at home. However, we know that many parents face external challenges that means they may require additional support. We must get this feedback from parents to form a partnership that will enable parents to play an active role in helping their child at school. This was illustrated by the Education Endowment Foundation report (2018) on parental engagement: 'It is important to talk to parents so that any plan is informed by an understanding of families' lives and what facilitates or impedes their support for their children's learning. By doing this you will, in your own school and contest, have a clear starting point from which to move forward.'

If we are to form partnerships with parents, we need to critically work with our parents. We should invest time in equipping our parents with feedback on how they can support their child in regulating their own learning and model this to support its implementation. For example, if we share the science of learning with pupils and teachers to support learning, we should also share this with our parents. Alongside providing parents with guides to support them, we can model how parents can support their child with learning at home. The emphasis here is to provide parents with guidance through modelling how they can help their child to regulate their learning. In one of the schools I worked in this involved an evening where there were a series of subject workshops covering the suite of qualifications on offer. Pupils and parents attended to work together on how to support their child to create regular routines and encourage effective home learning habits. This might include modelling to parents how to support their child with the following.

- Demonstrate how to create a revision timetable with their child to support spacing out revision.
- Provide time for parents to work with their child to use revision cards to retrieve knowledge.
- Make parents aware of the science of learning and generate an understanding of the most effective strategies that promote learning.
- Promote shared reading and engagement with the text through guided questions to support reflection.

Teacher Spotlight: Evolution of feedback

JAY DAVENPORT, PRINCIPAL

Jay Davenport is Principal of Manor School Sports College and has responsibility for leading the Nene Education Trust (NET) cross-trust leadership programme. He has accrued 24 years of teaching and leadership experience in five comprehensive schools that varied significantly in location, size and culture. Developing a particular interest in teaching and learning, curriculum, leadership development and wellbeing, Jay has been a senior leader for 12 years including five as a secondary principal.

Jay founded #NEDTalks as part of the grassroots Educating Northants movement, which is a teacher-led organisation promoting education, recruitment and CPD in Northamptonshire of which he is part of the steering group. You can find him tweeting as @jaydav20

At Manor School we have followed a path that I am sure has been well-trodden by many schools in the recent past and it started with the question: who is feedback for?

The past

Policy that is written in the offices of senior leaders is often dangerous as the very best of intentions can get distorted and the reality of the experience for staff and students is very different to the one intended. Sometimes in the drive to provide data for accountability to external agencies or the good intentions to reduce workload for staff, we forget about the end users and the people that support them.

In relation to feedback – or rather marking at the time – this type of centralised, whole school 'one size fits all' model created a system that worked very well for senior leaders and external observers who were able to track and monitor all manner of data which was rarely useful to inform learning. Consequently, it worked less well for staff and, most importantly, students and the parents who were trying to support their children. At best it ensured that leaders could check that marking had been completed. At its worse, it was a divisive system that disempowered subject specialists and was highly inequitable depending on how often you saw a group. Add into the mix various coloured pens for marking and processes for recording when verbal feedback had been given and a behemoth had been unwittingly created.

Policies such as this also proved problematic for parents who rarely saw books and were confronted with summative reports that were difficult to understand, meaningless or possessed identify issues that could have been resolved much earlier if they had been involved in the process more regularly.

The transition: focus on feedback not marking

We knew we wanted to include students and parents much more in the feedback process. An argument often presented for a one-size-fits-all model is that it is easier for parents to understand. What we discovered is that by engaging parents much more in their children's education through feedback, parents develop a good understanding of what is expected very quickly and are subsequently more engaged. In addition, we wanted to empower our subject expert staff and a whole staff wellbeing survey in 2017 identified that marking expectations had the greatest negative impact on wellbeing.

The first step in addressing this was to focus on feedback rather than marking. In doing so we wanted to visit a school that did this well and are particularly grateful to the staff at Tudor Grange, Solihull, for their input at this stage. We also wanted to identify general and subject-specific methodologies and to avoid the mistakes of the past by ensuring staff ownership of the systems that they were going to administer.

The current position

At Manor, we like to provide frameworks within which our subject experts work, enabling our staff to have the autonomy to develop subject-specific processes that follow the flow of their subject or course. This is true of curriculum and teaching and learning as well as feedback. Our teaching and learning framework 'Centralised Pedagogies' places feedback at the heart of the learning cycle. The whole school feedback framework provides a general statement about why feedback is important, a few checkpoints for summative collection of evidence and asks subjects areas to provide opportunities for formative assessment with feedback being provided to both students and parents.

Beyond this, each subject area looked at their curriculum content with fresh eyes and created a model of feedback that worked for them. This may look very different in mathematics than it does in design technology. The how often, what and when feedback would be given is bespoke to departments and influenced by the curriculum content and flow of the subject. Beyond the mechanics of the feedback structures, we have developed a series of walkthroughs (based on the original work of Michael Chiles!) that provide teachers with opportunities to reflect on how they use formative feedback effectively in their classrooms. Hinge questions, whole class feedback, live marking, questioning and sharing and reviewing learning intentions and criteria via a subject-specific good pass benchmark are all aspects utilised by curriculum areas within the formative assessment process of our whole school.

Centralised Pedagogies framework

Our subject specialists have developed criteria to create our subject-specific benchmarks. These criteria are the subject-specific skills that we feel students need to develop over their Key Stage 3 journey to achieve a 'good pass' at the end of Key Stage 4. Our benchmarks are used formatively to gauge a student's progress at a moment in time.

Teachers are engaging in informal formative assessment and feedback every lesson, every day. In addition, three times a year – at the appropriate time in each subject area's curriculum – formative dialogue between teacher and students concerning the subject-specific assessment criteria is completed and recorded. This dialogue is a deliberate opportunity for teachers and students to discuss the criteria, which the student is meeting, going beyond or still developing. Together, the student and teacher will identify what is currently going well in this area of learning and the actions to take to move further forward. This conversation is recorded on a simple radar graph that takes seconds to complete, is printed on bright orange so they can be easily found and stuck into books. The important part about the process is that this record is sent home for another conversation between students and parents. This means that parents are encouraged to look at students learning in their books on at least three occasions. It also means that, rather than giving a vague numerical grade or letter on a report, students have specific, individualised actions to work on and parents know what they are, enabling them to support.

Moving to our benchmarked formative assessment has had a very positive impact on summative assessment. We have been able to remove written subject reports that were completed annually. These reports took a lot of teacher time to write and middle and senior leader time to quality assure, often with very little impact. Instead, students and parents get purposeful feedback throughout the year at the appropriate time for each subject. This has also meant that our summative assessment has been able to be much clearer and precise, providing parents with the raw percentage a student received on a summative assessment and reporting a summative judgement of whether this is perceived by the curriculum leader as demonstrating expected progress since the student's starting point.

Problems along the way

To arrive at our current position, we have been through several iterations, walking alongside middle leaders and teaching staff to evolve our processes to ensure efficiency and effectiveness. Our good intentions of creating a feedback system that was effective and efficient for students reduced workload for staff and engaged parents. However, it did not immediately present itself in the format described and we have encountered and overcome several problems along the way to reach this point.

Problem 1: regimented whole school timescales. In short, our initial framework was too regimented on timescales. After initially setting three-week windows for their completion, subject areas used the benchmark points to 'record and report' progress, meaning that these points became summative indicators of the work completed until that point. The importance of the feedback conversation to improve learning was lost with students and parents using the information as a point they had reached rather than as a checkpoint of learning across the key stage.

Solution 1. To solve this, we have removed the windows for completion and subject areas have identified the appropriate moment to provide formative feedback in their schemes of work. This also reduced the burden of conversation on parents so that they did get 12 books and feedback to read and respond to at the same time. Instead, over the year, students take their books home when it is appropriate and will have the most impact in the subject area. This provides much more regular, structured feedback to students and parents based within the shared framework.

Problem 2: cost and benefit ratio of process. Initially, formative assessments took a long time to embed and quality assure correctly. Some teachers completing them in isolation, some were having lengthy, detailed conversations with every student, some were writing very long comments on the sheets. We were in danger of just replacing one behemoth with another – different system but still taking valuable learning time away in favour of an elongated assessment process. Our desire for short, sharp, informative checkpoints was not being realised how we had hoped.

Solution 2. Over time, through sharing of good practice and examples, staff now deliberately teach students a specific language for feedback that enables them to identify which criteria they are meeting, exceeding or developing. The deliberate practice of this particular domain in each subject means that students get better at making judgements about their own performance and can self-correct more accurately and more frequently. Through this, there develops a sense of student and teacher assessment with formative comments agreed together.

Problem 3: parental expectations. The idea of providing feedback using formative assessment points to enhance educational dialogue with students and engage parents much more in the process, formed quite early. One of the hardest challenges that continues to exist is changing parent perception of feedback. The education community is well aware that feedback is not the same as marking, but this is not the case for parents. Parents will often expect that every piece of work that their child produces deserves to be marked. Traditional 'marking' of a piece of work may take place but not every piece of work will or needs to be marked.

Solution 3. Teachers are becoming clearer at being specific about which pieces of work will receive feedback, the method that will be used and when this will take place. This is communicated and shared in a variety of formats, both in longer term planning and at the time the feedback occurs. Parent forums on the feedback process in school have helped shift perception and we aim to respond quickly to the feedback we receive from parents, both good and bad, about our processes.

The feedback received has been excellent. Parents/carers have commented on how they enjoy seeing the workbooks and reviewing the work completed. They report that the work over time, punctuated by the formative assessment feedback sheets, enables them to monitor improvement and enter into dialogue with their child or the teachers about progress. For example, parents know the books that their child is reading and the themes they are exploring, with some reporting that they are reading the books alongside their child so they can engage in more meaningful dialogue. This is a vast improvement on the previous system where they were reporting that they had lost touch with what their child was doing at school, often having been heavily involved during the primary school phase.

Next steps. The global Covid-19 pandemic has forced us to review our practices in many areas of our work. Some of this is restrictive however, there are also great opportunities for us. To this end, we are looking at how we can capture the new ways in which we have been forced to work in the areas of home learning, new and emerging technology and enhancing parental engagement, particularly with our hardest to reach families to develop even more effective feedback.

Key takeaways

- When schools work with parents to support children's learning indicates the crucial role parents play in supporting their child's learning.
- Despite the positive correlation between parental involvement and pupil outcomes, the degree to which parents and schools engage effectively in supporting children along their learning journey varies considerably.
- In many schools the feedback parents receive from teachers is often in the format of information giving.
- Parents' evening could be more effective through GROW conversations to move from parental involvement to a greater emphasis on forming a partnership with parents.
- We must get this feedback from parents to form a partnership that will enable parents to play an active role in helping their child at school.
- There can be a tendency to assume that parents know how to support their child in learning at home.
- Alongside providing parents with guides to support them we can model how parents can support their child with learning at home.

Chapter reflections

Use the space below to reflect on your own experiences of giving feedback to parents.

Chapter 4 references

Education Endowment Foundation (2018) ' Working with Parents to Support Children's Learning: Guidance Report'. Retrieved from: www.bit.ly/2UIhbZC pomegranate

Goodall, J. and Montgomery, C. (2014) 'Parental involvement to parental engagement: a continuum', *Educational Review* 66 (4) pp. 399-410.

Williams, B., Williams, J. and Ullman, A. (2002) *Parental Involvement in Education.* London: Department for Education and Skills.

CLOSING THOUGHTS FROM JOHN HATTIE

This book started with the observation that feedback is all around us. Sit in a class and observe a teacher in action and you will hear so many questions seeking feedback answers from students (typically involving less than three-word responses by students), skim through the papers the teacher has graded and you will find an abundance of feedback comments, and count the feedback utterances to students as the teacher walks around the class. As Chris Moyse says, we are so often rated and graded, criticised, and praised. We also receive and give feedback from peers, we are asked for feedback on most apps, we are given feedback from our bosses and often 360-degree feedback from those around us. Indeed, we could argue we are overfed on feedback and many of us may have a feedback obesity problem. We take it in, but do we process it appropriately?

So much of this frenzy of feedback adds little, is too rarely used to improve, is more about me than about what I am aiming to aspire to, invokes emotions that can led to diluting the information in the feedback, and many times we end a feedback session thinking, 'well that did not help'. Every evening at the dinner table, I would ask my (then) school-age boys, 'What feedback did you get from your teachers today?' It took them up to a year to understand my question and the intent was to make them appreciate that there is so much feedback and at minimum (to move to another more exciting topic), they had to listen to at least one feedback comment a day. On average, despite the thunderstorm of feedback from teachers, students receive about three to five seconds of feedback a day.

This book starts from the premise that it is not increasing the amount of feedback that matters but increasing the effectiveness of feedback that matters.

The question is less the amount and more why is feedback so variable in its effectiveness. We may be teachers who are keen to hear feedback to confirm the impact we have on our students, or we may be teachers who seek feedback to improve our impact, or both. The former tend to look for feedback that confirms their prior beliefs (and contrary feedback we can attribute to the deficiencies of the students, or their misunderstanding of our intent); the latter seek the negative and the positive as it is the negative they wish most to attend to as it is more likely to lead to improvements. That is, like students, some teachers look for confirmation whereas some look for improvement (and the best look for both). Moreover, we can receive feedback we do not know what to do with it, we can misinterpret or misunderstand the meaning of the feedback, we can avoid feedback as it can cost (we may have to do the task again, learn more than redo it) so it is sometimes easier to be a selective listener and not hear the feedback. Too many children by the age of eight learn the skills of selective listening. We know, for example, that when teachers give feedback to the whole class, each student knows it is not about them.

This book works from the premise that we need to understand the variability of feedback and understand the recipient of the feedback and how they receive, block, misunderstand and use or not the feedback.

The major message of this book is to consider feedback from the perspective of the receiver of the feedback. This means knowing the receiver, creating a climate of trust between you and the receiver, being seen as credible and trustworthy in the eyes of the receiver, showing that your intention is feedback aimed to improve and not to denigrate the receiver, nor hurt or harm, and most important to have social sensitivity so that you can know whether the feedback given is heard, understood and actioned. Unless feedback is actioned, it is just information, another set of advice floating in the wind.

This is a tough ask, should you be responsible if the student does not action your feedback. Yes, if you are a teacher (or a parent). More often, we need to stop and listen to how students hear, understand and action feedback. For example, after investing a Sunday in commenting and grading work, hand it back, wait a day (so it is not merely short-term memory), and then ask the students to jot some bullet points or sentences about the feedback you have provided. Look at their responses relative to what you provided and it can help show you the extent and depth of understanding the recipients have of your investment in their work. It can be sobering when they claim to have no recall, misunderstand it, interpret the wrong priorities, and see the feedback about them as people and not about how to improve their work. This activity can also provide you with information that can lead to improving your feedback to students, as surely we want to maximise the feedback that leads to action and improvement. If feedback falls in a classroom and no one hears it, did it make a sound?

My prediction is that where you provided feedback that aims to improve their work (telling them 'where to go next') then this will lead to the highest form of recall. Not that other forms of feedback are not valuable, but unless it aids action it is unlikely to be seen as valuable. If you wrote much praise about the student (e.g. about their general dispositions to the work, praised the person, or commented on the effort) or made negative praise this will be dominant in their recall. Praise too often dilutes any recall of feedback about the task and thus often dilutes the messages about improvement. If you provided underlines, ticks, '?' or other symbols, these will be most confusing as students often cannot intuit your thinking and meaning.

This book is full of ideas and techniques to maximise the student interpretation of your feedback so that it is heard, understood and actioned.

The major messages across this book beg for each school or district to develop a feedback contract or policy – for the school leaders, teachers, students and parents. Such a contract can help support a receptive feedback culture and promote the notions that feedback is not merely up-skilling those who give the feedback but also enhancing those (students, teachers, parents, school leaders) in receiving the feedback. Feedback is too powerful to get wrong. We need to consider teaching students how to be evaluative thinkers so that they can seek, hear, interpret and action feedback. We need to ensure that we get the feedback message right in the minds of the recipients, that we have an obligation to maximise the interpretation and use of feedback, to learn from this maximisation the best ways to provide feedback, to teach each other how we interpret and use feedback to improve, and to create high trust and safe learning environment for all this to occur.

This will move the debates away from how to give feedback, whether it is more valuable to grade or provide comments, whether the feedback is oral or written, the proper time to give feedback. We need to learn the lessons in this book on teaching students to interpret and action feedback, to see feedback as a benefit and not a cost, by listening to how your feedback is received and actioned. When we have provided teachers with feedback about their talking to students in a class, many are surprised to see they talk (on average) about 80-90% of the time in a class, how 90% of their talk is about facts, how nearly all their 150-200 questions a day require less than three-word responses by their students. They all too rarely see themselves through the eyes of the learners preferring to reflect on what they meant not what they did. Reflection is not looking in the mirror, it is seeing yourself through the mirror – more *Alice in Wonderland* than *Dorian Gray*.

This focus on receptivity soon moves to the emotional and affective aspects of feedback. It can hurt and it can bolster, it can be taken personally or can be seen as cold, and it can inject excitement and appreciation. As an academic, one of the rare gifts is when a colleague provides critical feedback aiming to improve my work before I send an article to a journal or before I teach a class – these critical friends are too rare. It is sometimes safer to not be critiqued and I certainly still feel emotions when my article is rejected – I regale at the misinformed reviewers, the incompetent editor, but then put the review in a drawer for a month before returning to the reviewers' comments realising that I could have fixed most of the problems with more effective writing. So, it was me! If only I had received this feedback from a colleague before sending the article in for review in the first place. As Michael writes, feedback = feelings, or feedback can be 'effective and affective' to the learner.

Negative affective reactions can lead to important feedback being ignored, negatively impact on motivation, confidence, engagement, and can reinforce any prior beliefs that I am not a good learner. Kluger and DeNisi (1996) showed that feedback that does not discourage ($d=0.33$ effect-size) and does not threaten self-esteem ($d=0.47$) was significantly more impactful than feedback that discourages ($d=-0.14$) and threatens self-esteem ($d=0.08$). Dylan Wiliam (2007) has argued that how a student responds to feedback will mediate whether they choose to pay attention to it or ignore it, increase or decrease effort, or decide the learning goal is too hard. Thus, feedback can carry a cost and the receiver often weighs up this cost in choosing to ignore, interpret, and action feedback. This cost can be highly influenced by the credibility of the giver, the attributed beliefs about the intent of the giver and the emotion invoked by the feedback.

This is a major reason why we have recommended that praise (about self or effort) is divorced from feedback about the task – as the formed can dominant, disguise or misalignment the power of the feedback as the receiver is so much more influenced by the emotional reaction about them. Imagine going to a doctor and she says you have disease X, this does not then mean you are a bad person but too often students hear they have failed an assignment and hear the message that they are bad learners. No, on this assignment the teaching could have been more impactful, the feedback more effective, the tasks clearer, the scoring or grading criteria more exposed to the student earlier as well as skills of the learner more enhanced. In this case, feedback could have been more situational, more task-dependent, more focused on improvement, and an important part of teaching is to prepare the student for failure, for summative feedback, for learning from failure. Michael Jordan, the GOAT of basketball, was so right: 'I've missed more than 9000 shots in my career. I've lost almost 300 games. 26 times, I've been trusted to take the game-winning shot and missed.

I've failed over and over and over again in my life. And that is why I succeed.' This brings meaning to the claim in this book: improve the learner, not just the work. Failure needs to be a learner's best friend.

For any pendulum, there is a sense of time or period, and now is the time to swing from the current focus on giving to receiving feedback. Yes, it is both, but this book is pushing us to provide much more focus on the receiver upswing of feedback.

References

Kluger, A. N. and DeNisi, A. (1996) 'The effects of feedback interventions on performance: A historical review, a meta-analysis, and a preliminary feedback intervention theory', Psychological Bulletin 119 (2) pp. 254-284.

Wiliam, D. (2017) 'Learning and assessment: a long and winding road?', *Assessment in Education: Principles, Policy & Practice* 24 (3) pp. 309-316.

CPSIA information can be obtained
at www.ICGtesting.com
Printed in the USA
JSHW040349020622
26362JS00002B/4